PENGUIN BOOKS

DEAD SILENCE

John Grigsby Geiger was born in Ithaca, New York, in 1960 and was educated at the University of Alberta, where he graduated in history. Based in Alberta, he is historical investigator for the Knight project and co-author of the bestseller *Frozen in Time*.

Owen Beattie PhD was born in Victoria, British Columbia, and is Professor of Anthropology at the University of Alberta, Canada. He was principle investigator for the Knight project. He is married and lives in Alberta with his wife and three children.

DEAD SILENCE

The Greatest Mystery
in Arctic Discovery

JOHN GEIGER and OWEN BEATTIE

Penguin Books

PENGUIN BOOKS
Published by the Penguin Group
Penguin Books Canada Ltd, 10 Alcorn Avenue, Toronto, Ontario, Canada M4V 3B2
Penguin Books Ltd, 27 Wrights Lane, London W8 5TZ, England
Penguin Books USA Inc., 375 Hudson Street, New York, New York 10014, U.S.A.
Penguin Books Australia Ltd, Ringwood, Victoria, Australia
Penguin Books (NZ) Ltd, 182-190 Wairau Road, Auckland 10, New Zealand

Penguin Books Ltd, Registered Offices: Harmondsworth, Middlesex, England

First published in Viking by Penguin Books Canada Limited, 1993

Published in Penguin Books, 1994

10 9 8 7 6 5 4 3 2 1

Copyright © John Geiger & Owen Beattie, 1993
Photographs © Owen Beattie, pages 1 *bottom*, 2 *top*, 3, 4, 5, 6 *top*, 6-7 *bottom*, 8;
John Geiger: page 2 *bottom*; Manitoba North National Historical Sites, Canadian Parks Service: page 1 *top*; Don Palfrey:
page 7 *top*

Title page illustration: Detail from Governor James Knight's Journal (1717, Hudson's Bay Company)

Canadian Cataloguing in Publication Data
Beattie, Owen
    Dead silence
Includes bibliographical references and index.
ISBN 0-14-016701-3
1. Knight, James, d. 1720? 2. Archaeological expeditions - Canada, Northern.
3. Arctic regions - Discovery and exploration - British. 4. Great Britain - Exploring expeditions. I. Geiger, John, 1960-
II. Title.
G650 1719.B43 1994   917.19'4041'092   C92-095734-X

FOR K. WARREN GEIGER & W. M. GILCHRIST - JG
FOR LYNDA - OB

In darkness, the Path.
- Brion Gysin
The Process

CONTENTS

Preface

Of all the tragedies which stud the pages of Arctic exploration, none is more poignant than the fate of James Knight's expedition of 1719. Little known outside specialist circles, the story is a bizarre and haunting one – of an aged veteran of the fur trade taking two ships and forty men from England into the icebound waters of Hudson Bay on a doomed quest. Guided by Chipewyan maps and reports from his years at York Factory, and with his ships rumoured to be carrying iron-bound chests to hold gold, Knight was in search of 'Yellow Mettle' and of the fabled Strait of Anian which would take him to the western sea.

After the ships left the Thames in June 1719 no member of the expedition was ever seen again. Over the years wreckage and Inuit reports pointed to Marble Island, twenty-five miles off the north-west coast of Hudson Bay, as the graveyard of the Knight expedition. Among Knight's former colleagues in the ranks of the Hudson's Bay Company suspicion grew that 'Every Man was Killed by the Eskemoes', and a sense of foreboding hung over the slooping voyages north from the Company's bayside posts for decades to come. The discovery by Company whalers later in the century of the final resting-place of the Knight expedition, at a shallow harbour at the eastern end of Marble Island, with ruins, sunken vessels and human remains, increased the sense of bafflement and horror. In the 1970s confirmation of a wintering came when investigators surveyed the remains of a substantial building at the harbour dating from Knight's time; but only in the last few years has a full-scale study been made of the expedition.

Working both in the archives and on Marble Island itself, Owen Beattie and John Geiger have combined scientific skills and historical imagination to reconstruct the story of James

Knight and his obsessive search. They have scrutinized every scrap of documentary evidence, and have matched this with four seasons of land and underwater investigation at the harbour on Marble Island. Much has been found at that ominous site, and a sounder interpretation of many aspects of the expedition is now possible; but the central issue of what happened to the forty men of the expedition remains as much a puzzle as ever. In a sense, the mystery has deepened, for as readers will discover, Marble Island is not giving up its secrets easily.

Glyndwr Williams,
Queen Mary and Westfield
College, London

January 1993

Authors' Note

Quotations taken from primary journals and narratives retain the original spellings and punctuation, rather than having been 'corrected'. Terms such as 'discovery' and 'the unknown' are used advisedly in describing the exploits of European expeditions in the Arctic. It is self-evident that aboriginal peoples 'discovered' the region centuries earlier. The word 'Eskimo' is a European invention, possibly based on an Algonquian word meaning 'eater of raw meat', and is widely viewed as pejorative by the aboriginal people of the eastern Canadian Arctic. We have chosen instead two terms: 'Thule', referring to the culture, now vanished, of the people first encountered by Europeans in the region, and, in reference to the area's historical inhabitants, the term 'Inuit', meaning simply 'the people'. Inuktitut terms in common English usage, such as 'kayak', are not italicized. Imperial measurements are retained in quotations; otherwise measurements are given in metric values, save for a ship's carrying capacity or when related to aeronautical convention.

Hudson Bay and position of Marble Island

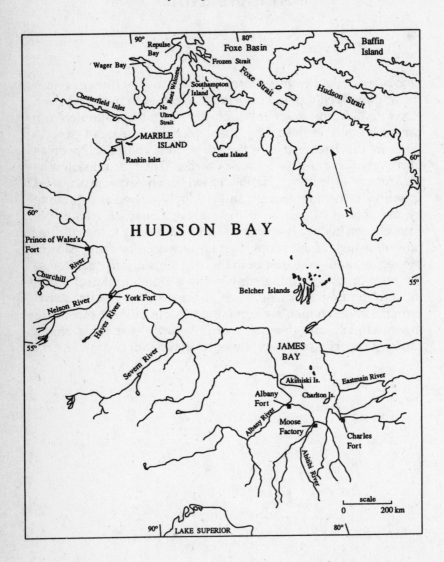

Repulse Bay — Foxe Basin — Baffin Island — Wager Bay — Frozen Strait — Foxe Strait — Hudson Strait — Chesterfield Inlet — Ross Welcome — Southampton Island — Ne Ultra Strait — MARBLE ISLAND — Coats Island — Rankin Inlet — HUDSON BAY — N — Prince of Wales's Fort — Churchill River — Belcher Islands — Nelson River — York Fort — Hayes River — Severn River — JAMES BAY — Akimiski Is. — Eastmain River — Albany Fort — Charlton Is. — Albany River — Moose Factory — Charles Fort — Abitibi River — scale 0 200 km — LAKE SUPERIOR

90° 80° 60° 55°

Marble Island

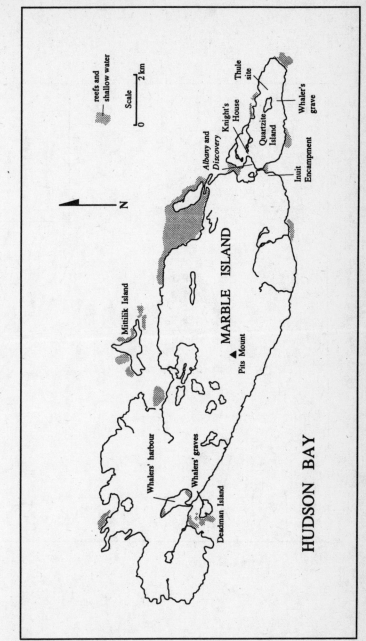

N

Scale

0   2 km

reefs and
shallow water

Thule
site

Whaler's
grave

Knight's
House

Quartzite
Island

Albany and
Discovery

Inuit
Encampment

MARBLE ISLAND

Mitiliik Island

Pits Mount

Whalers' harbour

Whalers' graves

Deadman Island

HUDSON BAY

Knight expedition site

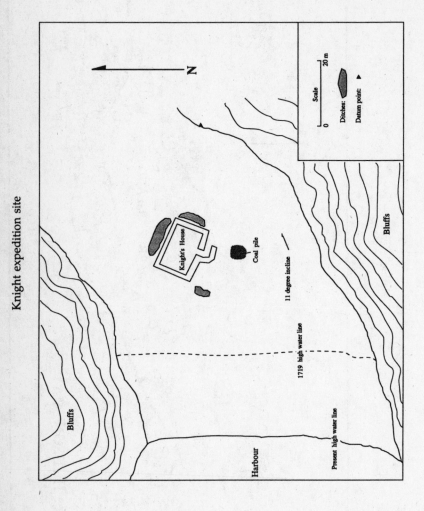

Bluffs

Bluffs

Bluffs

Harbour

Knight's House

Coal pile

11 degree incline

1719 high water line

Present high water line

N

Scale

0   20 m

Ditches:

Datum point: ▲

Map attributed to Captain James Knight, altered to show true orientation of coast

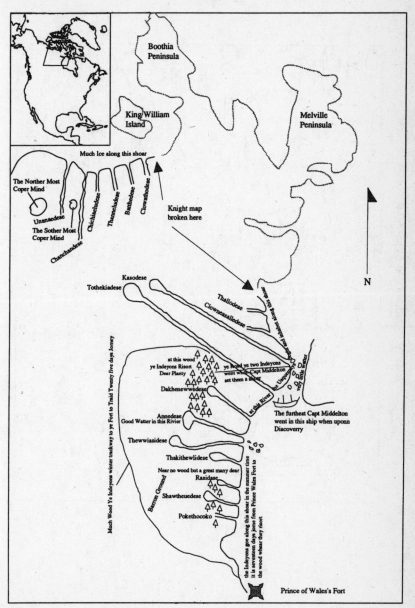

Boothia
Peninsula

King William
Island

Melville
Peninsula

Much Ice along this shoar

The Norther Most
Coper Mind

Unanaedese

The Sother Most
Coper Mind

Chichiachudese

Thanuchudese

Bathudese

Clowathodese

Chanchandese

Knight map
broken here

N

Kasodese

Tothekiadese

Thallodese

Clowneassilledese

at this wood
ye Indeyons Risort
Dear Planty

ye found ye two Indeyons
went when Capt Middelton
set them a shoar

Dakhenewwedese

Annedese
Good Watter in this Rivier

at this River

The furthest Capt Middelton
went in this ship when uponn
Discoverry

Thewwiasidese

Thakithewlidese

Near no wood but a great many dear

Rasidase

Shawtheuedese

Pokethocoko

Much Wood Ye Indeyons winter trackway to ye Fort to Traid Twenty five days Jorney

Barron Ground

the Indeyons goe along this about in the summer time
it is seventeen days jorne from Prince Wales Fort to
the wood wheare they risort

Prince of Wales's Fort

Places of significance to Knight and Hearne

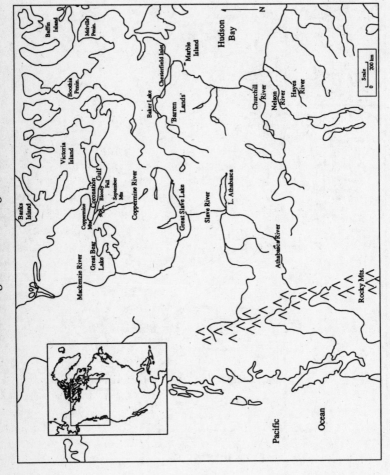

1

The UNHAPPY SUFFERERS

In the brief Arctic summer of 1767 the *Success*, a tiny Hudson's Bay Company whaling sloop, steered into the waters of Marble Island and the uncharted depths of human despair. The north-west coast of Hudson Bay was utterly unfamiliar, and thus, wholly malignant. It was a dark place, not only for geographical knowledge or the severity of the climate, but also for the spirit; a realm that one whaler warned 'would frighten any man, & Especially a Stranger'. As the sloop drew near the island's pale curtain of stone, no one was aware that they had reached the point where, half a century before, Captain James Knight had found the darkest place of all.

The *Success* was awaiting a rendezvous with another Company sloop, the *Churchill*, but the ship's prey were plentiful and the hunt would not wait. At dawn the next day, 22 July, Master Joseph Stevens sent out his boats. Ten arduous hours were spent in pursuit of twenty bowhead whales, but the animals were so shy the harpooners failed to get a fair strike at any. The men instead turned their attention to Marble Island and the collection of driftwood. Spying a narrow opening along the south-east coast, they prised in the boats. There, to their astonishment, they discovered 'a Harbour where there has been vessels a wintering'. Instead of baleen and blubber, they returned to the *Success* with three cannons and a smith's anvil.

The next morning Stevens braved a stiff gale and made for the new harbour with the small boats to investigate the mystery.

Landing at a break in the stone at the cove's limit, he ordered his men to survey the site, and 'to take particular notice whether there was any Letters or figures to be seen'. The master fixed his attention on the ruins of a large structure where the unknown expedition had wintered. There was something ominous. Its misshapen bulwarks, bound in moss, resembled a great burial mound. Scattered about were hundreds of bricks, appearing as fresh as if they had been made the previous year. More puzzling was the discovery of a large heap of good burning coal, which Stevens judged at seven or eight chaldrons (9.1–10.4 cubic metres). Near by lay rotten sails, and on the smooth face of adjacent rocks, wood chips identified where carpenters had been at work. The wood came from ships' timbers, giving him 'Many Reason to Judge of her being Lost'. Larger timbers led the master to estimate the vessel at not less than 40 tons, while the shanks of several anchors of variable size indicated that more than one ship was involved. Despite the abundance of artefacts, there was nothing by which to judge its age or national origin, save the discovery of some leather shoes with broad, square toes and high heels that suggested to Stevens, 'ye appearance of French fashion'. They were, in fact, English shoes fifty years out of fashion.

Stevens returned to the hidden cove ten days later, this time with Magnus Johnston, master of the *Churchill*, and carrying hatchets and shovels in the hope of finding papers. Digging within the ruin, the men came across a floor 'ab^t 3 feet down . . . laid in a Workman like manner with Brick & Mortor'. But that is not all the shovels unearthed, for soon a human skull poked through the damp ground. The discovery left Johnston with the full horror of realization that 'those Unfortunet people has ben lost', but Stevens remained unconvinced. Stevens was described by Samuel Hearne, mate of the *Churchill*, as 'a man of the least merit I ever knew'; and the dim conclusions of his investigation would seem to confirm the assessment. Studying the skull, he concluded: 'whether Native or Christian is not to say'. In the face of all he had seen, Stevens convinced himself that at least one of the vessels to have wintered at the site had 'gone well off'.

For his part, Johnston returned to his sloop certain he had viewed remnants of a doomed ship and crew. The proximity of the huge heap of coal to the entrance of the ruin suggested the crewmen had endeavoured to make a defence against the cold. The attempt at survival had apparently failed. Inuit interpreters gave Johnston further grim evidence of disaster: 'they heard there Country people Say that there Was some of ye English men Surviv'd the first winter – But wither they was Starv'd with could or hunger or Destroy^d by the Natives is a thing I cannot find out As yet'. The next day Johnston sent his young mate, Samuel Hearne, back to the vicinity of the grisly discovery to collect coal. Under a gloomy sky illuminated by lightning, Hearne and his crew began to dig. The sense of apprehension heightened with every scoop of their shovels. As Johnston later recounted:

> they had found A great Number of graves one of which Mr Hearne cawsed the people to Digg up in order to Sea if they find Any thing Remarkable – but could not – only the Bons of a Stout man who without Doubt is one of the Unhappey Sufferars.

Faced with the tangibility of death in such a disquieting place, the commanders shortly bore south for Prince of Wales's Fort with news of 'their great Supprise'. None yet realized they had stumbled on the remains of the 1719 Knight expedition and clues to a mystery as ancient and despair-provoking as exists in the annals of Arctic discovery.

Little by little, the nightmare began to unravel. When the whalers again converged at Marble Island in 1769, the relics had finally been identified as belonging to Knight's lost ships, the *Albany* and the *Discovery*. Hearne, already demonstrating characteristics that would soon make him one of the most remarkable figures in northern discovery, sought to learn more. Sighting several Inuit, one or two of them of advanced age, he interrogated them at length with the assistance of a Company linguist. Incredibly, Hearne gained a detailed account of the last days of the doomed expedition, a gruesome tale of the lingering deaths of forty men by illness and starvation. Even at the end of the first winter, in 1720, 'the number of the English was greatly reduced, and those that were living seemed very unhealthy'. In the summer of 1721, when the Inuit again visited the island, they discovered only five expedition crewmen alive. The ragged band of survivors devoured raw seal meat and whale blubber purchased from the natives, but 'this disordered them so much, that three of them died in a few days'.

Hearne's record of the fate of the last two survivors persists as the most haunting vision of failed discovery in the pageant of Arctic exploration:

[They] survived many days after the rest, and frequently went to the top of an adjacent rock, and earnestly looked to the South and East, as if in expectation of some vessels coming to their relief. After continuing there a considerable time together, and nothing appearing in sight, they sat down close together, and wept bitterly. At length one of the two died, and the other's strength was so far exhausted, that he

A stirring Victorian depiction of the last Knight expedition survivors, Marble Island.

4

fell down and died also, in attempting to dig a grave for his companion.

It was a merciless death; one of hideous, slow torture. Bodies inflicted with 'sickness and famine', drained of hope and will, living only for the horizon. But is it true?

2

A POINT of DARKNESS

Laid waste and silent on Marble Island, a place the Inuit came to call Dead Man's Island 'by so many Englishmen Perishing on it', is all that remains of Captain James Knight's rich dreams of 'Discovery of a Gold Mine in Terra Borealis'. Sealed there for nearly three centuries are not only the waistcoats and looking-glasses Knight hoped to trade for gold and copper ore, and the strongboxes, bound with iron, to hold the expected treasure, but also the secrets of the destruction of the first Northwest Passage expedition never to return from those frozen shores.

The pall endures to this day. From a distance, the wind-parched, rounded crests of white rock rise from Hudson Bay like a burial shroud. Inuit legend recounts that the island appeared suddenly, and that it was forged from the ice. All who go there must first crawl up the rock-strewn shore on elbows and knees, for fear that death will otherwise befall them. In July 1989, as the research team from the University of Alberta assembled in Rankin Inlet, a settlement located in the eastern district of the Northwest Territories recently declared Nunavut, an Inuit elder eyed each with a hard, piercing look, and spoke in Inuktitut. The translation sent a chill up the spine: 'You must crawl.' Every crew member did crawl up the cruel shore, partly out of respect for the people of this northern land and their ancient traditions, and partly to honour the souls lost there two hundred and seventy years before.

It is impossible to view the circumstances that surround Knight's disappearance without a shiver of horror, especially

in light of the centuries-old allegations that Knight's chief ben-
efactor, the Hudson's Bay Company, had been glad to be 'rid
of those troublesome men', and the possible complicity in their
destruction of the Company's Governor of Hudson Bay, Henry
Kelsey. Hearne's theory of 'sickness and famine' may indeed
have been the tragic finale of the Knight expedition, but too
many questions remained unanswered. Not least among them
is whether James Knight would have died in such a way and at
such a place, within sight of the North American mainland and
just four days by sea from the fur-trading post he had founded
on the Churchill River.

Knight was unlike any of the other explorers who came into
Hudson Bay to probe the unknown for a Northwest Passage,
from the first excursion by the visionary Henry Hudson, to
the strange and dangerous voyage of Captain Thomas James.
Knight was a product of the New World, weaned on deer
tongues and dark beer on the edge of a northern sea. For
twenty years he had endured the region's harsh climate in
the service of the Governor and Company of Adventurers of
England Trading into Hudsons Bay; for twenty years he found
ways to adapt and thrive where others had failed. Through
his respect for the perceptions of the aboriginal people of
the region, Knight had overcome much of the ignorance of
Incognita, the vast unknown. It seems inconceivable that
Knight and his veteran commanders, embarking the very
year Defoe published his classic imaginative work *Robinson
Crusoe*, would themselves have become the pitiable realization
of castaways, sitting out two winters on the desolate outcrop as
one after another of their crewmen died; as if waiting, until the
loss became complete. Yet of all the discoverers to have been
drawn into the grim reaches of the Bay, Knight alone suffered
the point of absolute darkness, the place from which no one
returned.

Knight was lured by the recurring dream of the first explorers.
Voyages into those unknown waters were undertaken in the
spirit of Sebastian Cabot, who set out in 1508 with the object of
leaving 'no parte of the worlde unsearched to obteyne richesse'.
Yet it is only for the flicker of geographical knowledge, and

for their suffering, that they are remembered. The frail barks could find no passage to the Oriental lands of gilded riches; they glimpsed instead a frozen realm of startling contrasts of beauty and desolation, alive with polar bears, dancing columns of snow and strange celestial phenomena. Even the light was perceptibly different.

John Davis, mathematician, navigator, author, inventor of the Davis quadrant or backstaff and self-proclaimed 'shining messenger', sailed in 1585 to preach the peace of the Lord. Instead he returned to England preaching the strange effect of the summer light in the northern regions, the suffusion of which made it 'the place of greatest dignitie'. At the entrance to this unknown, the Hudson Strait, first reported by Martin Frobisher as the 'Mistaken Straightes', Davis saw the beckoning waters of the Northwest Passage, concluding that 'the passage is most certaine, the execution most easie'. A corresponding northern passage from the west coast, now California, had also made its first appearance on charts, as the Strait of Anian. An Augustinian friar, Andrés de Urdaneta, even claimed to have returned to Europe from the Philippines in 1556 by way of the strait. In fact, the expected link between the two remained a dream as one expedition after another limped home in failure.

In 1610 Henry Hudson finally succeeded in sailing through the strait that bears his name into a vast western ocean. The remarkable discovery of what came to be known as Hudson Bay was overshadowed by the appalling events that followed. Hudson believed he had discovered the passage to the Spice Islands, but his dreams of Oriental riches were quickly shattered by the bleak sight of the southern coast of James Bay. Instead of the sheen of pearls, Hudson was left to study 'the footing of a man and a ducke in the snowy rockes'. The master insisted that there must be a way to the South Sea from this labyrinth, but his crew begged to differ. At the end of a miserable winter, Hudson announced his intention to resume the search. That decision, coupled with rumours that he was hoarding a stash of food, proved too much for the desperate crewmen. Less than a week after leaving their winter harbour, mutineers loaded the master, his young son and seven others into a dinghy and cut them adrift, to face certain death on the desolate shores of Hudson's frozen sea.

The discoverer was lost but his discoveries were not. The ship was piloted home, although none of the ring-leaders survived the gruelling journey. With news that Hudson's tragic voyage had revealed a great sea and had encountered strong tides from the west, the voyages continued the following year. Thomas Button rubbed up against Hudson Bay's barren north-west coast, which evoked wistful memories of his native

Icebergs.

Wales. Further north, Button found a channel, proclaimed Ne Ultra, where tidal evidence of the Northwest Passage was encountered.

Royal Danish Navy Captain Jens Munk followed in 1619, but encountered only a winter of untold suffering. Voyages made in 1631, the immediate precursors of Knight's own, revived the promise. Thomas James and Luke Foxe sailed within two days of one another, each seeking the passage to the South Sea and glory, though not necessarily in that order. James's most notable achievement was the literary flourish with which he began his chronicle: 'Many a Storme, and Rocke, and Mist, and Wind, and Tyde, and Sea, and Mount of Ice, have I in this Discovery encountred withall; Many a despaire and death had, almost, overwhelmed mee.' Wintering in the bay that now bears his name, James further proclaimed: 'If it be our fortunes to end our dayes here, we are as neere heaven as in England.'

While the numbing cold of a Hudson Bay winter turned vinegar so hard it had to be cut with a hatchet, James's inkwell was apparently unaffected. He recorded the ensuing ordeal in great detail, describing having his hair shorn as it was frozen fast with icicles, and then how, little by little, his men suffered. Blood froze, bones froze, and finally life ended. When spring at last arrived, a makeshift cross was erected and the crew gathered at the graveside of four dead companions. James paid a final tribute with a poem:

The Winters cold, that lately froze our blood,
Now were it so extreme, might doe this good,
As make these teares, bright pearles: which I would lay,
Tomb'd safely with you, till Doomes fatall day.

Four months later James was back in England. He had failed to find the Northwest Passage, but he had found his reward: his lurid narrative became a best-seller. Luke Foxe also failed in his quest for Oriental pearls to adorn 'the Lilly necks of the most daintiest Ladies', but he did make significant geographical contributions, having sailed north of the Arctic

Circle to discover what is now Foxe Basin. Once again, hopes for the existence of a western passage were kept alive with observations of the height of the tides at Button's Ne Ultra.

It was there, off the north-west coast of Hudson Bay, that Foxe sighted an unusual island of a stone unlike any other he had seen during his explorations. 'The island is all of a white Marble,' he recorded in wonderment. His boat had to nose past a pod of forty whales, at first mistaken for rocks as they were 'lying there to sleepe'. Once safely ashore, Foxe's men found themselves enraptured by the whistles of shore birds and the distant chatter of Canada geese. Drawn up the shelves of stone, they came upon protected hollows with 'many water Ponds therein, and great store of Fowle, especially water-fowle'. Foxe's ornithological count included a sandhill crane, which he mistook for an ostrich. Also sighted was a caribou, which was chased by the ship's dog. 'One of the Quarter-Masters, followed the chase, and having neither Gun nor Lance, let him goe,' Foxe wrote. 'It may be, he tooke compassion when he saw the Deere shed teares.' Discovery's first light was at an end. It would be close to a century before another explorer would again attempt the Northwest Passage through Hudson Bay, and then that same strange island was to become Captain James Knight's marble tomb.

In all of Arctic discovery, the 1719 Knight disaster is rivalled only by that of Sir John Franklin's third expedition, one hundred and twenty-six years later, in terms of the totality of the defeat and the extent of the mystery. But much of the cloud of unknowing that obscured the truth of Franklin's destruction was lifted during four scientific expeditions undertaken by the University of Alberta forensic anthropologist Owen Beattie and his fellow investigators between 1981 and 1986. For the first time, the tools of forensic science were applied to investigating the fate of men who had succumbed during their attempt to discover the Northwest Passage. The remarkable conclusions, reached following the exhumation of the permafrost graves of three Victorian seamen on Beechey Island, at once forced a re-examination of time-worn historical theories about the Franklin disaster, and focused scientific attention on the most enduring of all Arctic mysteries: the fate of Knight.

Great obstacles would stand in the way of any attempt to build on existing accounts of the expedition's last days. By contrast with the Franklin expedition, no massive relief effort was launched at the time of Knight's disappearance. There were no searchers' chronicles, no discovery of tragic notes left by Knight's men and no trail of fresh leads. The sole attempt to explore Marble Island specifically for expedition relics, undertaken by the American polar explorer Charles Francis Hall in August 1864, failed even to reach the island. Nor was there any hope of finding perfectly preserved human remains or artefacts, protected from decay by the icy grip of permafrost. Marble Island boasts a severe, unforgiving climate, but there is just enough sun each short summer to thaw its frozen ground. More than any other factor, though, it is time itself, like winter's darkness, that has obscured the truth about what happened to James Knight at the place of his destruction.

Beattie knew this time it would be different, that the search would not be limited to the investigation of human remains. Only by combining a wide range of disciplines, techniques as varied as those applied by the police to criminal investigations, would there be any hope of casting new light on the disaster. While contemporaneous written accounts contain vital clues to Knight's destruction, history alone is not enough. The resulting interpretations are encumbered with the biases of individuals themselves caught up in the events. None is entirely satisfactory. Where the historical record is invaluable is as a source of insight into Knight's complex personality, and in understanding the development of the ideas that led to his quest, and his ultimate defeat. By initiating the investigation, Beattie sought to reassess the historical record by discovering new evidence from the expedition – physical evidence that could be used to test the accuracy and validity of the prevailing historical interpretations.

Theoretically there would be no better witness than the remains of the dead. Forty bodies, innumerable images and angles of death. Each a clue to what transpired; the calamitous signs of bodies in disarray, the studied peace of skeletal fingers folded against the pelvis. Yet the existence of graves would not in itself be of any greater consequence than the context of any human remains located, or indeed the complete absence of graves. Forensic investigations involve the search for and documentation of separate lines of evidence, and in the case of the Knight expedition, potentially just as significant would be the location and investigation of the wrecks of the *Albany* and the *Discovery*. From archaeological excavations of the ruined shelter, and consideration of additional sites interpreted from surface artefacts or associations with the expedition, it might be possible to develop an understanding of how the eighteenth-century explorers lived on Marble Island, their food, their work. It might also be possible to determine the length of time spent at the refuge, before the stillness and silence returned.

The evening of 17 July 1989 marked the beginning of a four-year journey on ground long untouched; a journey across a bleak, white landscape. Landscapes do not forget human experience, and with each step the research team hoped to move closer to understanding. That night, after making the critical, at times dangerous, two-hour passage by fishing yawl from Rankin Inlet, and then after having knelt, as prescribed by legend, to pay their agonizing debt to the island's unquiet spirits, Beattie and his small group of investigators first approached the sheltered harbour where the Knight expedition had found its final refuge. As they crossed the massive outcrop, the cove gradually spread out before them, ripples in the water pointing to a small break in the stone at its limit. There, barely discernible in a gentle slope of pale green not more than 300 metres away, lay the fallen, rounded form of Knight's last outpost.

The ruin was a shade darker than the surrounding ground, its true size indeterminable against the barren backdrop. The approach to the shelter was slowed by the descent of the quartzite embankment, its natural bastions formed by jagged shards of rock hewn away by frost. At the base of the outcrop, boulders were replaced by smaller rocks that served as stepping-stones in the cold water of the retreating tide. Soon they walked onto the ground of the Knight expedition and stopped, gazing at the structure from near where it was first seen on 22 July 1767, before the harpooners of the *Success* rushed back to the sloop to report their discovery of 'The Ruins of ye House'.

What remains most striking is its imposing size: 14.4 metres by 9 metres, with walls of stone and earth built up 1.5 metres. None of the other explorers who searched for a Northwest Passage left behind such a monument in the emptiness. The vegetation near the ruin is true Arctic tundra, the soft, dense membrane of caribou lichen interspersed with sedges, scattered dwarf willows and only rarely, cream-petalled Arctic avens. The surface slopes 130 metres from the harbour up to a small freshwater lake, guarded by rounded quartzite outcrops that skirt north and south. Everywhere is a sense of what gave the whalers 'great reason to think a ship has been lost here'. The pile of rotten sails is now gone, as is the vast heap of coal. But in a circle, where nothing has grown in nearly three centuries, remnants of the coal pile are still to be seen. On the surface near by lay a leather sole left by one of the expedition's sailors, freed from the ground by erosion from the run-off of melting snow. Perhaps the sole once belonged to one of the same leather shoes that had confused sloop master Joseph Stevens about the origin of the wreck by suggesting 'French fashion'.

The location of the ruin, on low ground between two stone bluffs, suggested that it had been designed chiefly for protection against the cold winds. Only gusts curl down, leaving the best measure of the wind to the stagger of eider ducks flying overhead. At the entrance to Knight's house, dug deeply into the ground on the south-west side, it was dead calm; the threshold to a lost age. Just how difficult it would be to cross that threshold was evident from the start. Eight days into a systematic archaeological foot survey there was still no sign of the graves of the expedition's crew, nor were there other clues to help explain the cause of the disaster.

The only significant memorial to Knight's shattered dreams remained the ruined shelter itself. From a distance, its thick, uneven walls of earth and stone resembled a Bronze Age fort, not the final refuge of eighteenth-century explorers. It was near the ruin that its true origins were revealed. Dozens of bricks still lay scattered about. Some, eroded over time, are slowly crumbling, leaving their red footprint on the soft ground. Broken glass and rusting squared nails littered the ground below the lichen and the shallow roots of dwarf willows. But there was no sign of the 'great Number of graves' discovered by the whalers, no headboards marking last resting-places along the nearby beach ridge, no stone-covered mounds. Carefully excavated pits selected at random across the site revealed only the butchered bones of caribou. It was as if the crews had simply vanished; the fact of their existence no more substantial than the hollow wind.

3

The LAST PLACE in NORTH AMERICA

Fragmented incidents emerge from the mist, each a deliberate step in a life that stubbornly insisted on its own significance. Every development seemed to have its own end, an immediate ambition. Yet together they carried James Knight to a confrontation with seemingly illusory images of distant wealth, and ultimately to his destruction. It was as if, like the commander of Captain Marryat's mythical Phantom Ship, he was determined to fulfil his doom.

At first there are only intimations about Knight's life. The precise date and place of his birth are unknown, although there is compelling evidence that he was, in fact, the forerunner to Robert Peary, Richard Byrd and the other American heroes of polar exploration. In a letter to Knight dated 27 April 1683 specific reference is made to his 'New England countrey men'. But in the subarctic wilderness the Puritan virtues of frugality, sobriety and piety were superseded by Knight's primary virtue, the shrewdness with which he managed his own interests over the course of his career. It began on 15 August 1676, when the *Shaftesbury*, a three-masted Hudson's Bay Company supply ship, came to anchor at the estuary of the Rupert River in James Bay and sounded her great guns.

The cannon fire was meant to herald the ship's arrival at Charles Fort, a tiny fur-trading post perched at the edge of a great northern sea. But the reports that echoed that day marked a far more significant event, the first arrival of James Knight in Rupert's Land. At the start it hardly seemed auspicious. A carpenter and shipwright in his twenties, Knight had signed on at £42 per annum for a five-year stint in the Bottom of the Bay. Like other early Bay men, his immediate intention was only to ward off the threat of destitution and then to save enough money to return home with a certain degree of independence.

The Company propagandist Thomas Gorst had painted a tolerable, if not idyllic, picture of life in the lucrative trade for beaver skins, the lustrous coat being highly valued as headgear for its water-resistant qualities. These early glimpses of Charles Fort contained descriptions of cosy log cabins, beer 'brewd there for our dayly drinking', and, during the long winter, large chimneys designed 'to keepe alwayes Summer within, while nothing but Ice & snow are without doores'. Gorst's imaginative account even contained references to gardens sown with peas and mustard seed, and pens with 'hens & hoggs which lived and did well enough'. As Knight quickly discovered, the reality was different. Such was his dismay at the first sight of Charles Fort that forty years later he still groused, 'wee had nothing but a Little place not fitt to keep Hoggs in'. As it turned out, the hogs did not need a home anyway; the Company's experiment with livestock was subject to fits of failure, and frost repeatedly took care of the garden. As for the toasty fire, as soon as the wood burned down and the flue was closed, the cabin filled with acrid smoke that, a Company servant later wrote, 'makes our Heads ake, and is very offensive and unwholsome'.

In his 1708 history, *The British Empire in America*, John Oldmixon described the post as, a 'mean fort . . . in one of the rudest Parts of the World'. For Knight, ambition eased the awful reality. At Charles Fort he had not only entered a moss-thatched shack, but the ground floor of what the Capitalist prophet Adam Smith included among the 'mean and malignant expedients of the mercantile system': the colonial monopoly. The Governor and Company of Adventurers of England Trading into Hudsons Bay, or simply the Hudson's Bay Company, boasted a Royal Charter giving it title to a northern fur-trading empire of seven million square kilometres. This was named Rupert's Land, and the grant included the land,

and mineral, fishing and trading rights to a dominion encompassing the vast drainage basin of Hudson Bay.

Although Knight spent his initial five-year tour of duty at the Bottom of the Bay slaving over the construction of new accommodation, his accomplishments were not limited to carpentry. Ambition propelled Knight's rapid rise through the corporate ranks. The first evidence of this surfaced when he was ordered by Governor John Nixon to carry out construction of a new fort at the Albany River. Unhappy with the choice of site for the post, Knight sent a letter by messenger to the Governor at his seat at Moose Factory in which he informed him that it was too far up the creek and vulnerable on all sides to enemy attack. Knight was surprised, but evidently not rattled, by the response:

> Instead of Altering his Mind he sent me a very Angry Letter & told me it was my Business to Obey & follow Such Orders as he Gave or Sent me & not to Expostulate with him. I was Still

Eighteenth-century wintering house in Hudson Bay.

Unsatisfyd & Travell'd to Moose River To see whether I could not persuade him off of his Resolution, but he gave me Such a Wellcome that made me go back Again y^e Next Day.

The post was built where the Governor had ordered, but just four years after Knight entered the Company's service, its governing London Committee, made up of luminaries such as the architect Sir Christopher Wren, met at the Golden Anchor tavern in Cornhill to consider names for appointment as Deputy Governor in the Bay, with 'Master Knight being in nominacion'. Knight was passed over, but he swallowed his disappointment, returning to London in the autumn of 1681 to impress the Committee with 'a good Account of th' Estate of the Country both Indians & Factory's'.

Company officials would have listened intently to Knight's report. Despite two centuries of English discovery in Hudson Bay, the concept of a sea route by the 'Bay of the North' to the vast northern forests of fur was not an English invention. The idea had originated in New France as a logical extension of the lucrative northern traffic in beaver pelts begun in the early seventeenth century. Initiated at posts in Acadia (Nova Scotia), the trade gradually extended through Indian brokers along the St Lawrence, and finally inland by the *coureurs des bois*, itinerant fur-runners who invaded the wilderness to outdistance Indian middlemen. Despite efforts to diversify the colony's economy, the French settlements remained highly dependent on the fur trade, and its dealers were well aware of the threat the upstart Hudson's Bay Company posed to their claims. At the time Knight delivered his report, the French were preparing to launch a challenge to its monopoly, which was an endeavour conspicuous only for its occasional brilliant tactical success amid habitual dereliction.

Having impressed the Committee as 'very ingenious and knowing in the business of our trade', Knight was rewarded by being named Chief Factor of Albany Fort, on the west coast of James Bay. He soon received a second commission, this time the appointment denied him two years earlier. Knight was made Deputy Governor at Hudson Bay. He was awarded all the perks of the position, an additional £30 a year, furnishings for his quarters at Albany, including 'a suite of Curtaines, a p. fine blancketts, a rugge, a bedstead & curtine rods, carpett, 6 chaires, 2 spanish tables matts', as well as permission to hire his young brother Richard 'to waight upon him'. In an age when great attention was paid to the distinctions of rank, even a Deputy Governor stationed at a log cabin in the northern wilderness might at least enjoy its pretence.

In May 1682 five ships were made ready at Gravesend for the voyage to Hudson Bay, but months of careful planning collapsed at the quayside. On the eve of their departure the

Seventeenth-century artist's impression of a beaver.

Committee confronted expedition officers with an oath against private trading, the exchange of personal property for fur in competition with the Company's interests. While others readily took the oath, the prohibition clashed with Knight's entrepreneurial instincts and he fought with members of the Committee. When it came to his own pocket, the confident Deputy Governor was ready to take on even the shrewd City financiers who served as Company directors. At one point an edict was issued that the captain of the *Friendship* 'doe not receive on board his ship Mr James Knight wthout a warrant from some of the Committee'. The rift ended the same day with the Company claiming 'ample sattisfaction', and Knight finally embarked for the voyage to Hudson Bay. But the damage was already done. Doubts about Knight's fidelity persisted, and a letter sent out on the next ship reminded him, 'we still beleeve you will not deceave us but will behave your selfe as it becomes you in our service'.

It is perhaps for that reason that Knight was passed over for the governorship when the post became available in 1683. 'They had Actually promised me the Government of the Country,' Knight griped. More to the point, 'I Did Expect 130 Guinneas.' The job went instead to Henry Sergeant, who arrived with an entourage that included his minister, his son and three man-servants, as well as a 'whole parcell of Women', including his wife, her companion Mrs Maurice and a maid – the first white women to venture into Hudson Bay. The lofty demeanour of the new Governor was not well suited to life on the Bay and soon alienated the Company's servants, prompting him to complain to the Committee about their 'mutyning caballing & Rayleing'. Not surprisingly, a bitter Knight, himself grumbling that 'Victualls & Drink & all yᵉ best was Converted too their Use', soon also fell victim to Sergeant's remonstrations.

Knight was packed off to London in September 1685 to face charges of private trading. Hauled before a tribunal two months later, he sharply denied Sergeant's allegations, which involved a bundle of furs shipped out the previous summer. As proof of his innocence Knight produced affidavits attesting to his upstanding character and undying loyalty. The Committee was unimpressed, but suspended the proceedings to await the expected return of Sergeant that summer. A letter to the Governor dated 20 May 1686 confided:

> your severe charge agst. Mr Knight we have inspected, who does deny the whole; how ever we give you Credence & therefore have not discharged him, nor shall we until your arrivall, & then we doe expect you will make that charge good agst. him.

Sensing the seriousness of his predicament, Knight used the delay to try to court favour by forwarding proposals that 'can save ye Compa. some thing considerable in their charges in Hudsons Bay'. The cost-saving measures were read to the Committee the following month and included recommendations for drastic reductions in the number of men stationed at the three posts at the Bottom of the Bay, Albany, Moose and Charles forts, from a total of eighty-nine to thirty-six. Economies were also to prevail over discovery as Knight lobbied against a plan to send Company men inland to increase trade. It was not so much conservatism as pragmatism. Instead of attempting to compete against the French *coureurs des bois* on their own terms, he argued that the job should be given to Indian allies hired 'to perswade & invite the Indians to come to the English Factories'. The proposals were referred for further study, and Knight resumed his wait for Sergeant's return and his own vindication. Neither would come in 1686.

The battle for Hudson Bay would not be fought with just coloured beads and blankets. Years of chronic neglect of French interests in the subarctic fur trade abruptly ended with the appointment of the Marquis de Denonville as Governor of New France in 1685. De Denonville was confronted with an immediate decision: either drive the English competition from Hudson Bay altogether or face the ruin of his colony's fragile economy. The Hudson's Bay Company had succeeded in diverting a fortune in furs from Montreal and was flush with profit. In 1684 the Company had started to share its bounty with stockholders by paying a hefty fifty per cent dividend. Two years later its empire was under siege from the south. De Denonville gathered his forces together under the command of a young Parisian, the Chevalier de Troyes, and his fiery lieutenant, Pierre Le Moyne d'Iberville. In the spring of 1686 thirty French troops and seventy *coureurs des bois* set off from Montreal in a flotilla of thirty-five canoes. Indian guides led the raiding party up the Ottawa River, to Lake Abitibi and the Abitibi River, Moose River and eventually their destination, James Bay. Caught napping by night-time attacks, Moose Factory and Charles Fort fell to the French with little resistance.

Sergeant's well-fortified base at Albany Fort was a different matter. Demanding the Governor's surrender and receiving no response, de Troyes began lobbing mortar shots at the fort. The first interrupted Sergeant's dinner, causing his wife to faint and barely missing a servant pouring a glass of wine. After a hundred and forty volleys had been fired, the attackers' shouts of 'Vive le roi!' were answered by 'hollow voices' from within the barracks. The muffled response came from the cellar, where the Governor and the entire English garrison cowered. When the barrage at last ended, a lone figure emerged from the palisades waving a white flag. Within a month de Troyes and his men had captured all of the Company's posts save York Fort, a new factory to the north-west, on the distant Nelson River. Worse still, a truce ordered by the two kings, James II and Louis XIV, was ignored by the fierce d'Iberville, who stayed on as France's Commander-in-Chief of Hudson Bay, proving a scourge to Company interests.

The defeated Sergeant slunk back to London in October 1687 amid accusations that his surrender was the result of 'ill Conduct perfidiousnesse & Cowardize'. As a result of his remarkable failings, Sergeant was handed a hefty bill by the Committee for the loss of their factories at the Bottom of the Bay. Yet despite his sullied reputation and the more urgent Company business at hand, including petitioning King James II to act on the 'Concerne of this Compa. against the French', Sergeant was allowed to press his long-standing complaints against Knight. After eleven years of service, Knight's relationship with the Company was severed. He did, however, get in the last word. While Sergeant had managed to 'gett me Remov'd by his false Reports', he had also managed to dispose of 'the Country and all that was in it toe the French', Knight said grimly.

It took the splendid light of the Glorious Revolution to warm prospects for the recovery of the Hudson's Bay Company's lost empire. The expulsion of James II and the accession of William and Mary to England's throne in 1689 put an end to the uneasy truce that presaged a continuing French presence in Hudson Bay. The new English king took a harder line against the incursions, and the London Committee celebrated that 'it hath Pleased Allmighty God to permitt a Wonderfull Change in these parts'. Emboldened by the formation of the Grand Alliance in Europe and the first salvoes of King William's War, a secret meeting was called to plot the recapture of Albany Fort. The Company's surprising choice as leader of the attack was none other than James Knight, who by simple virtue of being in London under a veil of suspicion had been left untainted by

Pierre Le Moyne d'Iberville.

the capitulation to the French. Knight, described as 'of London, Merchant', was now middle-aged and of more than modest means, for he met the condition that he first purchase £200 worth of Company stock as a pledge of secrecy, equivalent to more than two years' salary at the rate at which he was paid when he first joined its service. When told that Knight was waiting in the ante-room, the Committee voted unanimously to make him Governor of the Bottom of the Bay, a somewhat dubious honour given that all the Company's former posts in James Bay remained in French hands.

The Committee was entirely different from that which had presided over his dismissal five years before, but Knight had not changed. The same characteristics of fierce independence and enterprise that had drawn him into service on the frozen sea, now drew the Committeemen to Knight. But this time it was James Knight, not the directors, who held all the cards. He played them to great advantage. While listening to their entreaties, Knight appeared indifferent to the offer of command, telling the Committee, 'he had severall Concernes of his owne depending & therefore could not now give his positive answer, But would give them his Resolution in a day or Two'. It was 14 March 1692. Knight waited a full month before announcing his decision. He would lead the campaign, but only on his terms.

A second meeting was called for that evening to hear his proposals, among them a demand for a share in the spoils of war. The Committee had to decide which was less costly: its losses to the French or the price of Knight's services. They opted for the latter and William and Mary granted royal letters patent to 'our Trusty and welbeloved Capt. James Knight . . . Wee reposing speciall trust & Confidence in your Loyalty & Courage'. The commission as Governor and Commander-in-Chief empowered Knight to make use of all the force necessary to seize French ships, men, goods and effects. Instructions approved two days later by the Governor and Committee put Knight at the head of the most formidable fighting force yet assembled for battle in the Bay. A flotilla of heavily armed frigates, the *Royal Hudson's Bay*, the *Dering* and the *Pery*, was joined by the *Prosperous*, for a total of 213 men and 82 guns.

Sometime in the hours after sailing orders were delivered on 23 June, Knight boarded the *Royal Hudson's Bay* and the ships slipped their moorings. Two months later the flotilla arrived at the Nelson River for a briefing from the factor at York Fort. George Geyer passed on Indian reports that the French had deserted their posts in James Bay, 'burnt them & were gone for Canada'. Leaving the *Dering* behind, the main force continued south to an island near the estuary of the Eastmain River on the east coast of James Bay. The onset of winter forced Knight to abandon his plans for an immediate attack. Provisioned for twenty months, the war party's commander chose instead to lie in wait. The long winter was passed with mortar training, hunting parties and daily prayers for divine guidance. A massive memorial erected to the glorious undertaking was discovered on the island fifty years later. The wooden plaque celebrating 'ye government of Capt. James Knight' later found its way into the possession of the Company and was last seen in the office of one of its senior bureaucrats in 1910.

The English assault was finally launched in June 1693. Knight's force landed near Albany Fort and, Geyer's intelligence proving wrong, was greeted with furious fire from French cannons and muskets. The stiff resistance left at least two English dead and many others wounded, among them the captain of the *Prosperous*. Knight fell back to regroup, attacking again the following day. This time, the French guns were silent. With no sign of activity, Knight crept cautiously into the fort confines, only to discover the sole occupant to be a deranged toolmaker locked in irons. The disconsolate conqueror's spirits were revived only by the discovery of thirty thousand pelts in the fort's stores.

French accounts shed some light on the mystery of the garrison's disappearance. A ship that was to have brought provisions to the French had been unable to reach Albany in 1692. Many men starved over the winter, and the bulk of the survivors, twenty-one in all, had been forced to embark on an arduous trek to Quebec one month before Knight's appearance.

Of the eight left behind to guard the post, five had trudged off on a hunt, returning a few days later to discover bloodstains in the snow. The toolmaker had apparently killed the company surgeon and then sought to confess his sin in the outpost's chapel. When the pastor exhorted the man to own up to the heinous offence in the presence of God, the wretch pondered the matter for a short time, but instead chose to chop the chaplain's head into pieces with his axe. On learning this, the mortified hunters clapped the mad smith in irons – just as Knight's ships hove into view. After their brave initial defence of Albany, the five starving Frenchmen had tiptoed past the English ranks and escaped into the night.

Making the most of his role as victor, Knight vigorously cross-examined his babbling captive, but learned only that the long-departed French Governor was named Le Meux. The prisoner, 'a French man borne at Ange on ye River Loir', was finally loaded with the pelts aboard the *Royal Hudson's Bay* for the long voyage to London. While it was hardly a victory that would stand comparison with the spectacular triumph over the French at Blenheim won a few years later by Knight's contemporary, the Duke of Marlborough, a one-time London Governor of the Hudson's Bay Company, Knight nevertheless played it for all it was worth. News reached London with the ship's arrival, and on 30 May 1694 the delighted Committee addressed a general letter to Albany praising 'ye Prudent management of Govr. Knight and wee are the more Rejoyced to find that it hath pleased Almighty God to protect & presarve him from the assaults of the Enimie'. Knight was asked to remain for at least another winter, as 'wee aprehend Albany Fort secure soe long as you remaine in it'. More important than the excessive praise, and the commissioning of a new frigate, the *Knight*, in his honour, were the contents of a private note from the Committee which got down to the matter at hand, namely the payment of a £500 bonus in the form of a bond delivered to his attorney.

As it happened, Knight had still more pressing concerns. No longer interested solely in the collection of animal skins, his eye had caught the glint of something as ancient as northern discovery itself, the lure of 'Mines & Mineralls' that had first entranced English fortune-hunter Martin Frobisher while searching for a Northwest Passage more than a century before. Frobisher had sailed in search of the empire of the Great Khan in 1576, dreaming of gold and perfumed fields of spices. Waylaid instead on the east coast of Baffin Island, he giddily excavated tons of glittering ore convinced that it contained gold. Fortunes may tumble into some men's laps, but Frobisher was not to be among them; it was fool's gold, and Frobisher was the fool. Knight, for his part, had in the months preceding the recapture of Albany Fort conducted a geological survey along the east coast of James Bay, the East Main, discovering 'a Vein of Stones' and 'a whitish Mettle that Looks like Dull Pewter'. Spurred on by the Company's promise that 'wee shall never be backwards in promoteing & Rewarding' anyone responsible for mineral discoveries, Knight continued prospecting from his base at Albany.

At first glance, it appeared that Knight had repeated Frobisher's mistakes. The Committee informed the Governor that samples he had collected and sent home, 'altho they might promise well to your or any other persons eye . . . upon examination they prove onely sulphur & vanish in smoake'. But suspicions that the minerals discovered by Knight were actually very valuable were subsequently raised when a rogue alchemist made off with them. Knight was asked to send more samples, and to dig deeply into the earth as there was 'Reall Minerall in the Bowells thereof'. Primitive mining equipment was provided to assist in the excavations, although Knight was informed that gunpowder was principally used in mining for minerals. One Gottlob Augustus Lichteneger, 'a Saxon and a Miner', was subsequently hired, and undertook a largely futile, decade-long search for Knight's elusive vein of stones.

In August 1697, five years after his triumphant return to the region, Knight put his prospecting endeavours temporarily on hold, appointed a successor and boarded the *Pery* for England. He did so in the proud knowledge that the Adventurers of England were once again absolute lords of Rupert's Land. Thick fog in the Hudson Strait preserved the illusion. As luck would have it, Knight had an uneventful passage home, oblivious to the presence of the most formidable fleet ever sent by France for battle in the Bay, with d'Iberville once again at the helm. Ravaging ice and raging currents in the Hudson Strait mustered England's best defence. One French warship was claimed by the violent waters, and another badly damaged. A third was driven into the range of the *Hampshire*, which had been sent by the Company in response to rumours of an impending French attack. But d'Iberville eluded even nature's fury and made for the Nelson River in his flagship, the *Pelican*.

Arriving off York Fort on 3 September, the French vessel was greeted with a salute from the guns of the English garrison, which had mistaken it for one of their own. D'Iberville was plotting York's recapture when three mainsails poked over the horizon. Believing it was the balance of his fleet, he weighed anchor and sailed out to greet them. His signals were not returned. Instead, three heavily armed English warships bore down on him. The *Hampshire*, *Royal Hudson's Bay* and *Dering* appeared invincible: one hundred and fourteen guns to the *Pelican*'s forty-four. The battle that followed raged for two and a half hours and was a bloodbath, claiming hundreds of casualties. The most dramatic moment came at the height of the conflict, when the tattered *Hampshire* pulled alongside the badly damaged *Pelican*. Captain John Fletcher and d'Iberville each sent for a bumper of wine to toast one another's courage, and the occasion of the greatest sea battle in the history of Hudson Bay. Moments later, d'Iberville fired a final broadside and the *Hampshire* foundered with all hands.

Incredibly, the retreat of the *Dering* and surrender of the *Royal Hudson's Bay* left d'Iberville the victor. He wasted little time in claiming York Fort. While French gunners used the English flag for target practice, their commander-in-chief prepared his assault. Realizing York's defences would almost certainly be overrun, the Company's garrison hastily surrendered. The contingent tried to maintain face by parading out of the stockades with drums beating, muskets shouldered, banners waving – and their baggage dragging behind them. They marched past the French lines and into the bush.

It was not until the French returned their prisoners a year later that the Committee learned of York Fort's capture and of Albany Fort's isolation. France was in control of what one officer dubbed 'the last place in North America'. After a decade of wilderness warfare, the Company's easy hopes of reclaiming a kingdom had left only wretched disappointment. If the flash of cannon fire had illuminated anything, it was that the costs of war were far too great to be borne as an operating expense. Company officials looked up from their ledgers just long enough to commission once again the services of Knight, the only officer in a decade to have honoured its claims.

The Treaty of Ryswick, signed just after d'Iberville's capture of York Fort, had failed to satisfy the Company. Under Article VII of the treaty, England and France were to restore all colonies to whomever held them at the time of the declaration of war in 1689. The result should have been the surrender of Albany Fort by the English in exchange for the surrender of York Fort by the French. But bickering stalled implementation of the treaty terms in the Bay, and the document was scrapped altogether when the War of the Spanish Succession erupted in 1702.

Knight, now listed as 'of London, Gentleman', became one of few overseas officers ever to earn a seat on the powerful Committee. He struck an imposing figure in the Company's

D'Iberville's capture of York Fort in 1697.

affairs, combining an innate mercantile sense with practical know-how, using his experience as a shipwright to supervise the construction and fitting-out of its frigates, at the same time as looking after his own financial interests, such as when he snapped up twenty-four lots of unsold marten pelts at bargain prices, producing with little difficulty the price of £933. Such was Knight's new-found eminence that in 1703 he was called upon to meet other Committee members at London's Jerusalem Coffee House 'in order to goe up to the house of Peers to Attend the Duke of Marlborough'. Not all occasions were so auspicious, as Knight oversaw for the Company the purchase of everything from beds and rugs to garden seed, even taking it upon himself to study ways in which cows would best be sent to Hudson Bay.

In February 1710 Knight was elected to travel to Holland 'in order to Solicit the Companys affaires at the next treaty of Peace'. He was accompanied by Sir Bibye Lake, a commanding City financier who, as the Company's London Governor, directed its fortunes for three decades. From their base at the English Coffee House in The Hague, the emissaries, armed with a trunk of books and documents to fortify the Company's case, attended meetings with Marlborough and Viscount Townshend to pressure for restitution of its captured posts and land. Remaining at the negotiations for four months, Knight and Lake successfully lobbied for a clause that demanded, in the words of England's Secretary of State, 'all the places and Colonys possessed by the French in the Bay and Streights of Hudson be delivered up'. The Company's object attained, the two returned to London to await the signing of the Treaty of Utrecht, which took place on 31 March 1713.

During this period Knight suffered a series of unspecified medical problems, finally so serious that on 19 April 1714 a member of the Committee was requested 'to go down to Temple Mills & see in what Condition of Health Capt. James Knight is'. However, such was his recovery that when they met to authorize the commission for the Governor to take repossession of York Fort, known during the period of French occupation as Fort Bourbon, the choice was obvious. Despite being in his mid-sixties, plagued with recurrent ill health and facing the prospect of a comfortable retirement, James Knight this time took just a day to accept the offer.

The man preparing to return to Hudson Bay differed from the obsessively practical young man who had clawed his way up through the ranks of hard-bitten fur traders at the Bottom of the Bay. As always, Knight's list of eight demands looked after his own economic interests. The Governor's creature comforts were to be ensured with an annual salary of £400, a fur coat fit for his 'own proper Wear' and a beaver blanket for his bed. Likewise, should grateful French traders wish to bestow any presents on Knight for relieving them of their factory, he arranged that such gifts would remain 'for my own use'. But there were also demands from Knight that he be granted an unprecedented degree of independence from London, ensuring that he would not 'be Tyed to Orders or Instructions'. This was done with an eye to furthering what would soon carry Knight beyond his characteristic pragmatism and ultimately to his Arctic grave: the pursuit of 'new Discoveries', notably those of the mineral variety. Lest any of his fellow Committeemen consider his terms negotiable, Knight made it clear that 'upon no other I think to go'.

Accompanying Knight as deputy was Henry Kelsey. A quarter of a century earlier Kelsey had made far-ranging discoveries of his own after the Committee directed that 'the Boy Henry Kelsey be sent to Churchill River . . . because we are informed he is a very active Lad, delighting much in Indians Company, being never better pleased than when travelling amongst them'. The young apprentice was enraptured by the wilderness, becoming the first European to travel overland hundreds of kilometres north of the Churchill River. While in his early twenties Kelsey undertook a second, yet more marvellous expedition, travelling up the Hayes and Saskatchewan rivers in 1690–2 to become the first Englishman to reach the prairies of western Canada. There Kelsey gazed upon herds of buffalo, crossed paths with grizzly bears and wrote a tantalizing account in verse of his travels.

Kelsey's subsequent career was somewhat less noteworthy,

although while serving under Knight at Albany Fort he was awarded a £5 rise for 'his Fidelity and diligance in all respects'. He briefly captained the frigate *Knight*, and had risen to command a Company factory before, in 1714, joining Knight himself on board the *Union* and sailing for York Fort. Knight carried with him a Royal Commission bestowed by Queen Anne, who had succeeded William of Orange in 1702, authorizing her Governor-in-Chief in Hudson Bay, 'To take possesion for Us and in Our Name of the said Bay and Streights, Lands, Seas, Sea Coasts, Rivers, Places, Fortresses and other Buildings, Cannon, Cannon ball, Powder and Provision.'

For a time it seemed that Knight would be denied his triumph. A defect in the *Union's* steering mechanism resulted

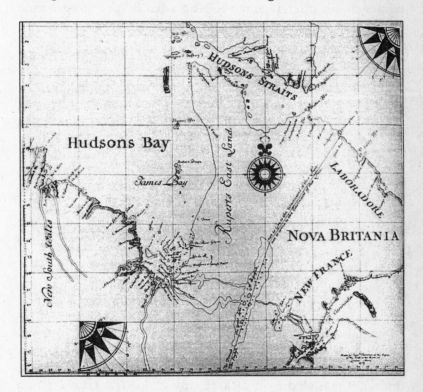

Map used during 1710 peace negotiations.

in a harrowing voyage through the Hudson Strait. The clumsy frigate was dashed against ice floes, then trapped in the ice for five days, at one point being carried perilously close to land. After a great struggle the *Union* at last broke free and in early September came to anchor off the headland that separates the Nelson and Hayes rivers at York Fort. Knight wasted little time in reclaiming the post. 'I sent my Deputy Ashore wth. ye Shallop with ye French Governs. Letters & Gave him the Queens Commission . . . to show the power wee had to take Possession of ye Place,' Knight wrote in the first entry of his York Fort Journal, a daily diary that survives as an amazing chronicle of northern survival and discovery. The significance of his literary undertaking was indeed not overlooked by Knight, who incited Committeemen to read what he promised would be 'a more particular account of your Country then yett you ever had'.

Kelsey returned the following day with Nicholas Jérémie, France's Governor at Fort Bourbon, to negotiate the exchange. A native of New France and veteran fur trader, Jérémie turned out to be every bit a match for Knight, squabbling over each detail of the post's surrender. After being rebuffed twice in his demand that Jérémie turn over the keys to the fort, Knight finally received possession and disembarked to survey his new seat of government. He did so with a dawning sense of horror, for 'ye Place as wee are come to is nothing but a Confusd heap of old rotten Houses without form or strength . . . my own Place I have to live in this Winter is not half so good as our Cowhouse was in ye Bottom of ye Bay'. The Governor would have only his beaver-skin blanket to keep him warm.

On Saturday 11 September the French Governor gathered his men and read them their marching orders. The French flag was lowered as Knight hoisted the banner of England. After reading his commission to the motley assemblage, the new Governor 'Proclaimed ye Queen wth. Usuall Ceremony', firing off the post's guns and toasting Her Majesty's health. While the French packed, the twenty-seven Company men celebrated long into the night, assisted by a cask of strong ale. The revelries had barely ended the next day when the Company's new clients arrived to hold council. One of the first Indians to venture into the reclaimed fort informed Knight that he preferred the French standard to the English, a reminder that after seventeen years, 'Many of the Indians has great Friendship for the french.' In his *Narrative of Twenty Years of York Factory*, the outgoing Governor went a step further, interpreting trade patterns established with the French garrison as evidence that they had been considered 'fathers and protectors' by the natives. 'The same attachment is not shown towards the English,' mocked Jérémie. 'They say they are too deceitful and that they never tell the truth, and this they do not like.'

Whatever the reason, Knight's first council at York Fort demanded 'a great Deal of Ceremony', with the Indians laying out tokens of friendship – beaver pelts, deer tongues and animal fat – on the ground before the Governor. Four calumets, or peace pipes, were then produced. It was to be a hard-earned peace. Knight complained that he was forced to take 'so many Whiffs out of Every Pipe' that he had ended up 'an Absolute Smoker'. The three-hour ceremony ended with the presentation of gifts to the natives, along with Knight's promise of fair dealing. The Indians were apparently left unconvinced and three days later the solemn ritual had to be repeated in its entirety.

In late September Knight ordered that the *Union* be made ready to sail, and three days later, with the French garrison aboard, the vessel began its long return journey. Among the cargo of French traders and their beaver pelts was packed a letter to the London Committee. 'This is to Congratulate you in the Possession of your Right in ye Whole Country of Hudson Bay,' Knight proudly informed them. The Company's sunless winter was finally at an end. For Knight, the darkness had only just begun.

4

The SLAVE WOMAN

Rationality does not fit comfortably with the single-mindedness of the quest on which Knight was about to embark. Its origins almost certainly lay in the prospecting and mining conducted after his recapture of Albany Fort. There is likewise evidence that Knight had taken up the narratives of the first discoverers, Button, James and Foxe, and pondered the possibilities of the ultimate land of gilded riches. His subsequent endeavours, though, more closely resemble Francisco de Coronado's misty-eyed wanderings of the American west in search of the golden realms of Quivira than the more precise exploits of those who searched for the Northwest Passage. Indian rumours had lured the Spanish captain-general deeper and deeper into the unknown continent, his conquest of 1540–1 eventually terminating in Kansas, where the only evident riches were in the endlessness of the land. For Knight also, the mineral riches lay not in a distant Oriental fiefdom, but within the unexplored realms of the New World, a region more interminable than anything Coronado could have imagined. That in mind, Knight had arranged not only the authority for exploration, or the necessary accoutrements, 'Cruseables, Melting Potts, Borax &c for the Trial of Minerals', but for a one-tenth share of any profits.

Believers prepare for affirmation, and during the first nights at York Fort, James Knight searched the black skies for a sign. By a strange chance, a Chipewyan woman at the fort delivered the awaited portent. The woman's eyes lit up at first sight of the old Governor, grandly decked out in dress indicative of his superior standing. She clapped her hand on his tunic's shiny gold buttons and announced that there was an abundance of such precious metals in the distant lands to the north-west. Sadly, Knight's hours of vigorous questioning proved too much for her to bear and 'it pleasd God shee Sickned & Dyed'. He was lamenting the loss when a second messenger mercifully appeared.

Referred to by Knight simply as the Slave Woman, the remarkable Thanadelthur had escaped a Cree captor and stumbled into the tent of a goose-hunting party at nearby Ten Shilling Creek. A Chipewyan whose band, the Slaves, lived on the distant shores of Great Slave Lake, she was captured in a Cree raid carried out in the spring of 1713. The Slaves derived their name from repeated raids suffered during the tribal conflict, in which the Cree had the upper hand because they were the first to be armed by English and French traders. Thanadelthur had intended to return to her own people by crossing the vast Barren Lands, but her attempt failed and instead she sought refuge at York Fort. Awed by her appearance as if from nowhere, and already respectful of the general accuracy of Indian counsel, Knight instantly realized that Thanadelthur would 'be of great service to me in my Intention'. Indeed, she was destined to be one of the most intriguing figures in the history of northern discovery, her life's experience and the shared knowledge of her people shaping how Knight perceived her country, its geography and its offerings.

Chipewyan oral tradition emphasized Thanadelthur's youth and attractiveness. Because both traits were likely to have been fleeting given the tremendous hardship imposed by the nomadic existence, and because strong, young women were prized captures in the tribal conflicts, it has been judged that Thanadelthur was probably in her teens when taken by the Cree. It was, however, her resolute character and intelligence that captivated Knight. The Slave Woman soon held the Governor spell-bound with rich tales of a distant country, a place where 'the rocks are of Diverse colour & by Description full of Mineralls', where there were 'plenty of

Martins Ermin fox Quequihatch & Buffelow &c', and where there existed 'a Large River or Streights that the tides Ebbs & flows at a great rate & yt. it hardly freezes some Winters'. To Knight this could only be one thing: the place of men's dreams, the Northwest Passage.

By January 1715 Knight's hopes for discovery had been temporarily replaced with persistent despair. Under the northern sun ice crystals can glitter like diamonds, but in midwinter at York Fort, night's gloom seemed endless. 'It is so black & Dark Cold & Whett,' Knight lamented, his bleak colony's winter routine interrupted only by partridge shoots and the occasional amputation of a frozen digit. With eighteen hours of darkness out of every twenty-four, Knight occupied himself with trivialities, studiously recording some of Canada's earliest weather reports and keeping an exact tally of daily partridge and rabbit kills. When it came to the hunt, the English proved no match for the French, Knight's totals falling far short of those claimed by Jérémie, whose garrison of eighty men had feasted

Interior of a Cree lodge.

on ninety thousand partridges and twenty-five thousand hares during the winter of 1709–10. The climatic data gathered in the daily journals provides a rare glimpse of the forceful effects of the Little Ice Age of 1650–1850.

Then at its nadir, the Little Ice Age made its fearsome presence felt in Europe at the end of the seventeenth century and throughout the first decades of the eighteenth. Cold, wet weather in Germany and Switzerland resulted in significant advances in Alpine glaciers. England experienced a winter of very heavy ice formation on the Thames. In an analysis of the conditions, climatologist Dr Timothy Ball writes, 'the severity of storms in this period is attributable to the extreme mean southern position of the Polar Front'. That the climate in the Hudson Bay region was considerably colder than at present is evident from Knight's repeated, gloomy descriptions of 'very freezing cold' and 'gales'. Ball has shown that York Fort, now located in the boreal zone, would then have been considered subarctic.

On 13 February 1715 misfortune ended the monotony. Two of the Company servants returned from an outing to report that a third man, George Mace, had collapsed in the snow from exhaustion. They wrapped him in a beaver coat and returned to the post for help. Knight immediately sent out a search party, and the following day ordered the post's tailor, Thomas Butler, to join in the effort. The searchers eventually came upon Mace's tracks in the snow. The trail led homeward for nearly a kilometre, then veered back towards the Nelson River. They followed the path to the banks of the frozen river, where they built a large fire and shot off several rounds. At about nine o'clock a blizzard set in, extinguishing the flames and forcing the disheartened searchers to retreat.

It was two days before Knight could send out another search party, this time consisting of Butler and two Cree guides. At noon came word that Mace had been located. Despite frozen hands and feet, he managed to drag himself to the spot where the fire had been set and had huddled by the dying embers. Another fire was built and Butler attended to Mace while the guides returned for a sledding crew. At last Knight was able to report, 'they brought him a^(bt) 8 a Clock at Night in a Misserable Condition with his hands swelld prodigously from his fingers End to the joint above his wrist and his feet much froze'.

There is nothing exceptional about Mace's suffering. A 1742 treatise presented to the Royal Society on the *Extraordinary Degrees and Surprizing Effects of Cold in Hudson's Bay, North America*, observed that despite bundling into winter dress that included deerskin shoes, breeches lined with flannel, fur caps, yarn gloves 'and a large Pair of Beaver Mittings', men who ventured out of doors in winter regularly returned with 'their Arms, Hands, and Face blister'd and frozen in a terrible manner, the Skin coming off soon after they enter a warm House'. Mace lost more than his skin. Three weeks after the rescue, Knight casually recorded that 'the armor. made an amputateing chisoll for George Mace hands & feet'. The grisly task was conducted over ten days, and on 18 March Knight observed 'now he hath Neither fingers & toes'. Less than a year in the Company's service at the time of his injuries, Mace survived the ordeal and remained engaged as an object of charity.

The tragic episode was not at an end. Haunted by the memory of the discovery of his frozen mate, Butler fell into dissolution. He held the Governor's strict 'Orders for the Mens Behaviour' in contempt. Knight's puritanical conduct code forbade, among other things, swearing, quarrelling, drunkenness, smoking in the storerooms and meddling with Indian women. It also required that the men 'do such things as you are ordered from time to time wth Cheerfullness & Willingness'. Butler exercised restraint only in the matter of smoking in the storerooms. After repeated warnings had gone unheeded, Knight convened a general council to deal with Butler's villainous practices.

Searching Butler's room on the Governor's orders, Henry Kelsey discovered loose floorboards concealing a hiding place. Stuffed there was a bundle of beaver and fox skins taken from the warehouse. Knight might have considered Butler a man after his own heart, had the hole not been dug so deeply into the ground adjacent to Knight's cellar as to allow frost to damage his personal liquor store. The furious Governor read Butler's crimes into the post record:

> Stealing Brandy out of my Chambers . . . Stockings Soap & a Beaver Skin from the warehouse and Provisions from the men and against my order lyeing with a woman of this Country to the Endanger of our Lives wch sev^{ll} of the french was killd for . . . at another time he likewise on my not letting him have brandy at his Demand he went publically amongst the men abuseing me Callsing me lyeing Old Rogue.

Butler was summarily convicted for his 'high crimes and misdemeanours', discharged from the Company and made a prisoner to be sent home on the next ship. But he did have the last laugh, making off with full wages in London before the Committee knew of his crimes, 'by Reason wee had not Time to Read the Gov^{rs} Journal it being so Voluminous'.

The loss of two men, one to the infirmary and one to the stockade, proved inconsequential alongside the other forces mustered against the Governor's eager hopes of success. While the Bottom of the Bay had been a place fit for man, York Fort had proven to be 'the Devill of a Place', wrote a bitter Knight. No sooner had the miserable winter ended than spring unleashed its own fury. Knight had just sat down for dinner on 7 May 1715 when, during the spring break-up, ice forced the Hayes River to flood its banks. The water rose so rapidly that the Governor and his company were compelled to scramble for safety, leaving 'all our Victualls standing on the table'. The entire garrison was forced to 'betake our Selves to the Woods', where they watched helplessly from the treetops as the torrent crushed the post's palisades.

Such was the force of the flood that it would not have mattered 'if St Paul's had stood there'. Chunks of ice accumulated around the structures that remained standing, creating ice mountains metres higher than the tallest building. The deluge appeared to have ended by nightfall, but the following day the water rose to yet higher levels. Knight's regular Sunday services were replaced with prayers for salvation. That night 'a very great Noise of Cracking & Rumbleing' left the men gripped with terror. 'This hath been a night of fear and pain least I should find in the morning all lost,' Knight scratched in his journal.

When the flood waters at last began to recede, the men returned to waterlogged quarters and the realization that the foundations of a new post would have to sit on higher ground. In what begins as an effusive letter to the London Committee lauding his boss's 'speedy care' in attempting to protect the Company's goods, the post's warehouse-keeper Alexander Apthorp ends with gloomy complaints of their 'wretched unhappy or uncomfortable life'. Such is the account of misfortune that Apthorp felt compelled to explain that the stains on the letter were not tears, but were 'from the droppings of the upper deck'.

With disaster barely averted, there came the renewal of hope that again extended to the discovery of mineral treasure. Knight seized on the opportunity afforded by the lull in misfortune, plotting to send an expedition on a peace mission into the Barrens, for until a peace could be forged between the warring tribes, his aim of new discoveries through an expanded trade with the distant Northern Indians – Knight's term for the Chipewyan – could not be achieved. In June 1715 the Governor hosted an elaborate feast for the 'Home' Crees and, speaking Cree, enquired how many were willing to give peace a chance. Only fourteen stepped forward, but the ranks swelled when Knight promised great rewards on their return. The volunteers were generously supplied with powder, shot and tobacco. Command of the expedition was nominally entrusted to William Stuart, a native of the Orkneys who had enlisted with the Company as a thirteen-year-old apprentice a quarter of a century before. Thanadelthur was to accompany Stuart as interpreter, although there is no question that hers was the commanding presence. Knight understood the importance of Thanadelthur to the success of his plan, instructing his emissary to ensure 'none of the Indians abuse or missuse the Slave Woman'.

In his instructions to Stuart, Knight emphasized that he

should make 'a Strict Enquiry ab^t there Mineralls', and also inform the Chipewyan of a plan to erect a trading post at the estuary of the Churchill River. His orders ended with a crafty reference to that most precious of commodities: 'if you find any Mineralls amongst them you must seem Indifferent not letting them know it is of any value but bring some of Every sort you see . . . Especialy some of the Yellow Mettle & Copper.' With that, and a bid for a successful journey, the Stuart expedition, with the Cree and their families numbering one hundred and fifty, left York Fort for the north-west.

No sooner had Stuart's column disappeared into the brush than calamity returned. The failure of Captain Joseph Davis to find the entrance to the Hayes River that summer forced the supply ship *Hudson's Bay III* to return to England without unloading its cargo. Knight heard the vessel's guns fire, but was unable to attract the attention of Davis, who, he fumed, mistook even a bonfire set on the shore as 'a Starr setting'. For several days Davis 'lay blundering', first to the north side of Port Nelson, then to the south. At last the ship's sails disappeared from view. Knight was livid on realizing that Davis had 'like a Thoughtless, Ignorant, obstinate fooll turnd tail & run away for England Again'. The Governor's rage did not diminish over time. In a letter written two years later he expressed disbelief that Davis had not thrown himself overboard, 'rather than go home with Such Shame & Dissgrace'. Knight expressed faint pleasure only with the news that the incompetent commander, fearful about having to explain his actions to the London Committee, had developed a severe fit of gout. Without the supply of provisions to sustain them, Knight's colony faced additional hardship during their second winter, but the event would prove catastrophic for the natives who had come to rely on the Company's trade for their survival.

In the months after he had taken back York Fort from the French, Knight made note that some Cree had sighted a Windigo, 'wch is an apparition'. These hideous monsters, with eyes 'rolled in blood' and an insatiable appetite for rotten wood, swamp moss, mushrooms and human flesh, were believed by the Indians to wander wraithlike in the northern bush, sometimes possessing the body of a man. Company factors routinely dismissed fears brought on by the visitations, one boasting in 1779 that 'a little brandy, properly applied, had a wonderful effect'. The beast's appearance was not so easily discounted by Knight. Often associated with times of starvation, in this instance it proved a harbinger of an artificial famine. When fleets of canoes began to arrive in the spring of 1716, weighed down with valuable cargoes of pelts, Knight was forced to explain that he had no goods to trade. There were no new guns, and there was none of the powder the Indians depended on for hunting. Without arms for their long trek inland, they were doomed to almost certain starvation. As a result, most simply refused to leave.

'I am sure wee are but in a badd Condition to have so many discontented Indians abought us,' Knight wrote on 1 June; 'wee lye in a Manner to there Mercy.' The English were especially vulnerable because the new post on higher ground remained largely unfinished, without its defences. Among other delays, work on the moat had been thwarted by the presence of permafrost, of which Knight composed the classic definition, observing that 'the summer never thaws above the depth of what the following winter freezes'. Knight counted more than four hundred canoes belonging to the Upland Indians alone. With an average of one hundred and forty skins per canoe, some quick arithmetic enabled the Governor to estimate that the season's trade would have already amounted to more than fifty thousand pelts. 'Such a trade there had not been the like for 20 years at this Factory.'

The scope of the mounting tragedy increased by the day. 'The Indians look upon themselves in a Manner [as] Dead Men,' Knight wrote on 3 June, horrified to watch suffering that turned strong young men to skin and bones. Many of the natives died as a result of the Company-instigated famine, although the exact toll will never be known. It is grim evidence of the degree to which the Indians had already become dependent on the fur trade. People whose ancestors had lived for centuries off the land were suddenly made reliant on goods from Europe for their very survival. Knight, unable to support the swelling numbers of natives with the post's dwindling supplies, responded by ordering veteran Company seaman David Vaughan and two others to make the long journey to Albany Fort by canoe to scrounge for provisions. Vaughan had only just left when the Governor's heart sank at the appearance of another thirty-six canoes, these belonging to the Mountain Indians: 'I am more Concernd for these than any as has been here yett by reason they come the farthest and border upon the worst sort of Indians in this Country that are their Enemys and I am heartily sorry.'

By August more than a thousand hostile, starving Indians were camped for 150 kilometres up-river from York Fort. A passing herd of caribou provided a brief respite as 'the Starvd troublesom gang as hath layn abt. us so long robbing & Plundering one another struck their tents & went away'. Within two days they had returned. Knight had his men working double shifts in the rush to complete the post's palisades. The English could not leave the confines to hunt or collect firewood in preparation for the imminent winter for fear their presence would incite an attack. Knight knew

Naive European depiction of a Cree canoe in Hudson Bay, with palm tree.

of an incident four years before when Jérémie had sent out a hunting party under similar circumstances. In his *Narrative* Jérémie writes that the starving natives were enraged by the sight of the French hunters gorging themselves on game. The Indians fell on them at night, cutting the men's throats at the moment of their waking, then making off with their weapons and powder. One of the hunters survived by playing dead, and the attackers contented themselves with stripping him of his clothes. When they left, he bound his wounds with the leaves of trees and began the long hike back to the fort, 'through brambles and thorns, as naked as an infant just born'. The man survived the ordeal, warning Jérémie to prepare the artillery against a raid. Knight received a similar warning, but from the Indians themselves.

An angry chief confronted the Governor on 22 August, warning him that 'all the Indians were very much exasperated against us for their Disapointment'. After delivering his blunt message the chief left, explaining 'he darest not Stay any Longer for he believed the Indians would come and attempt to do us a Mischief'. Knight immediately inspected the state of the construction work, noting 'thank God wee have 2 Sides inclosed with Pallisades'. The next day he called council with the Indians to announce that the supply ship from England would arrive within ten days. The bluff paid off, with Knight confiding in his journal, 'In the mean time wee shall be able to Inclose ours Selves and to defend us any attempts as they have threatened.' Seven days later the palisades were complete.

With characteristic modesty Knight proclaimed that the new fort provided 'the best and biggest house and flankers' in the country, although six years later a dour successor, Thomas McCliesh, dismissed York Fort as an 'Irish hut'. Behind the barred gates of his wooden fortress, Knight speculated bitterly on where fault lay for the failure of the ship to arrive the previous year, whether by the 'drunkenness & neglect of the commanders' or as evidence of a broader neglect by the Committee of its northern empire:

I don't know what to think but this I am sure the country is

46

worth takeing more care abt it than is done and I am Sorry when I confide how little the Company setts by the Country and looks upon it as a Dead Weight in there Estate when they have not such another flower amongst them when rightily mannag^d.

The long-time shareholder further complained that £1000 worth of Hudson's Bay Company stock could have been exchanged for £5000 in stock belonging to the powerful East India Company had only the Company not starved a good cause.

Then, after morning prayers on Sunday, 2 September, came what might have been a cannon burst at sea. Knight answered with one of York Fort's pieces, but he feared his powder was wasted. There was no reply and no ship was sighted. Next morning, while Knight was hosting a roomful of expectant Indians, seven cannon reports sounded offshore. 'The noise of the guns sett them a skipping jumping and Hallowing as if they were madd,' Knight wrote. The Governor was more

Ships entering the Hayes River near York Fort.

47

relieved than excited, noting 'there was never more occasion of a ships arriveing'. A veil of fog at last lifted to reveal the Company's proud frigate. That night the Indians celebrated their salvation by dancing with firebrands along the banks of Hudson Bay. Knight too danced, into the strange vagaries of desire.

5

PETTY DANCERS

The Stuart expedition's progress was slow. In a letter written the previous autumn but not delivered until April 1716 by some of the Cree who began to straggle back to the post, William Stuart reckoned he had travelled no further than 160 kilometres beyond the Churchill River. Stuart complained to Knight that he had not eaten for eight days, and sadly predicted, 'I do not think as I shall see you any more but I have a good heart.' Two of the Indians who had returned reported that the main party was sick, and so weak they could not hunt. Stuart was described as being 'in great fear of being starvd & weeps very much to think of there Misfortune'. The Indians said they had been forced to eat their dogs and had split into small groups to survive. Still, some of the Cree had succumbed 'upon the Barren Mountains'. Four days after receiving Stuart's letter three more Indians arrived at the post to report that after separating from the main party they had encountered some of the Northern Indians, whom they claimed to have killed in self-defence. Despondent about the news, Knight resigned himself to the mission's failure, promising, 'I must try for it again.'

Knight's spirits soon lifted. After 'a most Miserable fatigue', Stuart and his delegation arrived back at York Fort on 7 May 1716, bringing with them ten Northern Indians bedecked with glittering copper ornaments and a tale of terrible struggle into the uncharted depths of North America. More than fifty years before celebrated explorer Samuel Hearne made his own trek into the Barren Lands, Stuart too had adapted the customs of the aboriginal peoples, travelling north-west into the wilderness for about a thousand kilometres. Knight recorded that the expedition had traversed 'that Baren Desarts and when they crossd them they went WNW^t and came into a very Plentifull Country for Beasts'. It is one of the great feats of exploration, but it is unknown. Stuart was only semi-literate and unlike Hearne, brought back no written testimonial of his achievement.

The historian Arthur S. Morton estimated that Stuart reached the northern boreal forest south of Great Slave Lake and east of Slave River. There, according to Knight, he found the gruesome evidence that nine of the Northern Indians had been murdered by Cree members of his party. Fearing revenge, Stuart considered turning back. Thanadelthur would have none of it, persuading the delegation to wait ten days while she sought negotiations with the people of her country. In dramatic fashion, on the final day, the Slave Woman reappeared, 'hollowd and made her signall she had found some'. Stuart counted two others with her, but as he approached, Thanadelthur gave another signal and one hundred and fifty young Chipewyan warriors emerged from the brush. According to legend, 'when she beheld her people coming, she sang with joy'. Negotiations proved difficult, however. Hoarse either from song, or from her 'perpetuall talking to her Country Men in perswading them to come', the Slave Woman was unable to arbitrate. Instead, one of the Indian leaders pulled out a pipe, 'made a Long harrangie of the sacredness of that thing', then lit up. After each side had taken so many whiffs, he told them they were now to be lasting friends. When Thanadelthur's voice at last returned, she announced that a factory would be built at the Churchill River where her people could come to trade. Knight was ecstatic on hearing the news: 'By this success I beleive our Company may begin to be thought a rich Company in a few years and if it please God to preserve me with Life and health to go through with what I Design.'

In his report Stuart paid the highest tribute to Thanadelthur, informing Knight that 'he never See one of Such a Spirit in his Life'. He also expressed real fears for her safety. She had scolded the Cree the entire length of the return journey about the cowardly way some of their party had killed her people. Then, learning that one of her own kind had been found with a Cree woman, 'immediately Shee took up a Stick and beat the Man twill She made him Roar out'. Later, when an elder broached the idea of trading sub-standard pelts to the English, she 'ketcht him by the nose pushed him backwards and called him a fool'. Back at York Fort, even the Governor was subject to her wrath when he accused her of giving away a kettle that had been presented to her. '[She] did rise in such a passion as I never did see the Like before,' Knight marvelled, adding, 'I cuffd her Ears for her.' Some modern studies have decided that Chipewyan women ranked lower in the social order than in any other tribe, and were considered little more than 'pack-animals'. They have not read of the Slave Woman. To her own people, Thanadelthur had earned considerable respect for her service as agent with the English, with whom they opened a trade for cherished goods. To Knight, Thanadelthur was much more than merely his chief instrument in attaining the peace, for: 'Indeed She has a Divellish Spirit and I believe that if thare were but 50 of her Country Men of the Same Carriage and Resolution they would drive all the [Southern] Indians in America out of there Country.'

The Governor was not beyond paying small tribute to his own great ingenuity either, observing that the money spent to bring about the peace 'is the best layd out of any as ever was in the NW^t'. Proof of this was worn by the Northern Indian newcomers, whose rings, bracelets and knives glittered with copper. Knight was now firmly convinced that 'the Beaver trade only will never make the Company very rich'. The future was in metals. He eagerly questioned the strangers, recording that 'there is found great Quantitys of pure Virgin Copper lumps of it so bigg that three or 4 men cant lift it'. While enticing, copper was not all that Knight sought. Rather, he exclaimed, 'thare is a Parcell of Indians as lyes upon the west Seas as has a Yellow Mettle as they make use of as these do Copper'. As Knight's excitement grew, so did the descriptions of the mineral wonders. The Governor was, as the post's surgeon John Carruthers later put it, 'very earnest in this Discovery,

51

which was always his Topic, and he took all Opportunities of making Presents to the Natives'. The largesse was exchanged for accounts of copper mountains, outcrops of silver and islands of gold.

While the treasure was certain, the geography was less so. Knight had to grapple with confused descriptions and rough maps drawn by the Northern Indians. Even so, they provided him with a greatly broadened field of vision. The elements were incorporated into an entire system of geographical perception: limitations on apprehension about what lay beyond the Barren Lands were overcome through the eyes of people who had come from there. It was no longer an uncharted land. Remarkably, one map, attributed to the hand of the Governor himself and based on geographical descriptions provided by the Chipewyan, was sent to the Committee in London and as a result has been preserved, excepting alterations made in reference to Prince of Wales's Fort and the later voyage of Captain Christopher Middleton. The simple map, with its geographical features recorded in Chipewyan, affords a rare glimpse of the unique geographical perception on which Knight based his subsequent endeavours. It depicts the vast stretch of coastline extending north from the Churchill River in Hudson Bay and all the way to Coronation Gulf, beyond the mouth of the Coppermine River on the Arctic coast, but neglects the westward change of direction of the coast in the area of Boothia and Melville peninsulas.

The map specifies the location of several copper mines near a river, and the name of the sixteenth river, the Chanchandese, or 'Metal River', identifies it as the Coppermine. In his journal Knight recorded the existence nearby of 'great hills and Mountains' of the mineral – probably a reference to the small ranges of the Coppermine and September Mountains. Along the banks of the river itself, huge lumps tumbled out of the cliffs. Here Knight's intelligence has proven remarkably accurate. A 1972 survey of the area's geology identified eighteen localities, stretching for hundreds of kilometres in the Coppermine area, where native copper occurs in usable amounts, as slabs, sheets, thin leaves and kidney-shaped conglomerates. As early as the fourteenth century, natives were mining the deposits, and archaeological sites in a great radius from the Coppermine River have revealed examples of copper hunting implements and tools such as stemmed knives, awls, punches and needles, as well as decorative items like bracelets and beads. As late as 1929 a geologist for the Canadian Department of the Interior discovered a massive 273-kilogram nugget in the area.

Of the rivers north of the Churchill, one was believed to be the elusive sea passage to this land of riches. But the story seemed to change from day to day. On 11 May Knight recorded, 'I could not hear by them that thare is any Straights that parts Asia from America.' The very next day he writes, 'I begin to think there may be a Passage or straits.' Indeed Knight wanted to believe, and took as confirmation an account from one Indian who maintained he had been to the country of the Copper Indians, a name given the Yellowknives. He gave a vague description of a large river that 'comes out of the West Sea'. At the bottom of this river was a great bay with three islands almost out of sight of land, and 'them Indians [that] Inhabit thare brings a Yellow Mettle'. In this case, at least, the 'sea' that beckoned was not the Pacific, but probably nothing more than Great Slave Lake. The source of the yellow metal cannot be precisely identified, but could relate to any of a number of proven gold deposits in the north-west. Still, the geographical intelligence gathered by Knight was considerable, and the natives even spoke of 'Gum or pitch that runs down the river' – the earliest reference to the Athabasca tar sands. The timely arrival of other Indian parties added to the great picture, which now included an account of the existence of a land where mountains rose almost to the sky. By making a record of this, Knight provided what is arguably the earliest European description of the Canadian Rockies.

The Governor was more interested in what was supposed to lie beyond the mountains: a wealth of precious metals. He learned of a tribe of Mountain Indians who 'garnish themselves with a White Mettle and hangs it in their noses and ears'. A woman who had been among the Crow Indians helped corroborate the tales by enticing Knight with claims that on a western sea coast lumps of gold were washed from cliffs in heavy rains. 'Her Eyes had seen it and her hands had fellt it,' Knight rejoiced. Because great trees were said to grow along it, the west coast was judged not so cold as the east part of America. The sea was open to shipping, Knight decided, and each year the Indians 'see Sev[ll] Ships in the Western Seas wch cannott to be Spaniards . . . I rather take them to be Tartars or Jappannees Vessells'. Strikingly similar tales were told to Knight's immediate predecessor, Jérémie, who was informed not only of the existence of a rich deposit of native copper, but also received strange accounts from the Indians that, after several months' travel to the west, they had encountered a great sea where large ships carried 'men who have beards and who wear caps, and who gather gold on the shore of the sea'. Jérémie had likewise received reports of northern straits, which he too concluded to be the Northwest Passage.

Knight's confusion over geography was exacerbated by attempts to reconcile the geographical perceptions of the Indians with the misconceptions formulated by European cartographers. In his eyes the problem was made worse because of his 'great Oversight' in lending a copy of the northern explorers' journals to a fellow Committeeman in London. Knight complained that, because the borrower had promised to return it on the eve of his departure for York Fort but had failed to do so, 'I must now make all the Discoverys in the dark for want of it.' It is unclear just how the early narratives would have helped. Two hundred years of European discovery had failed to determine the existence of a passage through the north-west coast of Hudson Bay. On the Pacific coast of America, explorers had not yet reached north of what is today the coast of Oregon. It would not be until 1741 that a Russian expedition under Vitus Bering sighted mainland Alaska. Spanish naval officers explored the unknown coastline of British Columbia in 1774 and 1775, while the great navigator Captain James Cook searched for a Northwest Passage along the west coast in 1778. In May 1716 Knight was stationed at the edge of the known world. His remaining years would be dedicated to finding a means of entry into the Earthly Paradise that lay beyond.

Faced with the dilemma of how best to obtain the riches, either 'by trade or a Vessell', Knight first opted for the techniques he had successfully employed during his long tenure with the Hudson's Bay Company. Believing it was 2400 kilometres across 'from Sea to Sea', and uncertain of the location of the sought-after straits, Knight chose to trade. He sent samples of 'Naturally Virgin Copper' to the Committee in London, seeking to learn its value and customs duties and predicting a profit margin of three hundred per cent. When the Committee responded a year later, it was to inform Knight that copper 'from our own Plantations' paid no customs duty, and 'could you procure a Quantity either Oare or otherwise it would turn to a better accompt than skins, so hope you will Encourage that trade as much as you can'.

Knight hardly required encouragement, having proceeded nonetheless without official sanction. In the intervening months he had informed the Northern Indians that 'I would make them chisolls to cutt them great Lumps', and renewed his pledge to move further to the north and west, establishing a fort at the Churchill River 'that they may gett wt Copper & other Comoditys they can to come & trade there'. To ensure the easy passage of mineral-bearing canoes, efforts were next made to extend the peace 'in the whole Country Round from N to SW^t'. Native envoys were sent in all directions bearing small gifts and messages of reconciliation, for if peace were established, Knight decided, it would be 'the first as hath been made amongst them since the Confusion of Languages at Babell'.

The elaborate plans remained unfinished. Knight placed the blame for the collapse of his carefully crafted strategy squarely on the shoulders of Captain Joseph Davis, that 'harebraind Crazy fellow' who was unable to find the entrance to the Hayes River and deliver his cargo. Because they had been forced to wait until late in the season in 1716 for supplies before making their arduous upland treks, many of the Indians failed in their attempts to reach the distant lands. The Crow Indian envoys who headed for the western sea were reported to have starved. 'I was not able to Supply them Sufficiently to carry them through,' recorded an aggrieved Knight. The Chipewyan who remained at York Fort suffered because the Indian threat had kept Knight's men indoors during the brief goose-hunting season. All were forced to subsist on the paltry provisions that were finally delivered by the frigate in September 1716. English cooking bred rampant illness among the Northern Indians. Acknowledging that the daily fare of oatmeal, bread and dried partridge was 'not fitt for man to putt in his Belly', Knight experimented with having some of the Chipewyan billeted with the resident Cree. The attempt largely backfired. One Northern Indian boy crept away in the night and made the

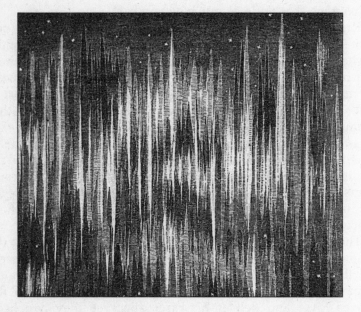

Nineteenth-century attempt to capture the splendour of aurora borealis, Knight's 'petty dancers'.

eight-day journey back to the factory to report that they 'took away all yᵉ things as I had given to keep him in the Winter as he was afraid they would take away his Life too'.

The cruellest blow was yet to come. On 8 December 1716 Knight noted in his journal that Thanadelthur had fallen ill. Three weeks later he observed that the aurora borealis, or 'petty Dancers', were 'Exceeding bright and flew about very much'. The remarkable curtain of light that undulated across the Arctic sky held Knight entranced. Perhaps he even heard the muted whistling to which they were supposed to dance. But in their splendour Knight saw something else, the pale face of Death. The evil omen was fulfilled days later when he recorded that 'the Slave Woman Lyes Exeeding Ill and very Light headed wᶜʰ I thought she would have Dyed to Day'. Soon three others were similarly afflicted, including the boy who had returned from the bush. Knight personally nursed the invalids, moving the Slave Woman and the boy into his own bedchamber. Exhaustion from worry over their condition affected his own health, resulting in frequent fainting spells. 'I have Sometimes been allmost Crazd by laying it so much to heart & [it] has been the Main Cause of my Sickness,' Knight wrote on 30 January 1717. Five days later Thanadelthur was dead.

With the passing of the Slave Woman, Knight saw the beginning of the end of his dream of reaching the treasure of El Dorado through trade. His journal entry for that day, 5 February, begins with gloomy observations about its implications for his grand design. But, for once, Knight was touched far more profoundly than in his pocketbook. Thanadelthur was, he said, 'endued with an Extraordinary Vivacity of Apprehension'. He credited her with having been 'one of a Very high Spirit and of the Firmest Resolution that ever I see any Body in my Days'. Even on her deathbed, she called for a Company apprentice, Richard Norton, who was to have accompanied her on the journey home that summer, encouraging him to continue their important endeavour, and 'not to be afraid to go amongst their Indians for her Brother & Country People would Love him and not Lett him want for anything'. Knight led a burial ceremony at four o'clock and gave out to survivors 'a few odd things to these for to Wipe away their Sorrow'. He then divided up her possessions according to her instructions. At the end of the day Knight collapsed in grief: 'I am so concernd for her Death and for fear of the rest so Dangerously Ill as they bee that I am almost ready to break my heart . . . Oh Davis, what has he done by his Ignorance & Folly.'

On 22 February another Northern Indian died. Helpless against the fierce fever that afflicted them, Knight was driven to desperate measures. Rhubarb, 'Purging Pills' and 'the Elecutarys Conserves Powders' were to be administered to the sick. Fearing the environment within York Fort's barracks had 'partly Suffocated us all' and had exposed the northerners to 'Stinking Lamps . . . & Unholesom Smells', he moved the infirm to a tent erected outdoors. Two men were posted to care for them round the clock, but the fresh air did not help. On 25 February the boy died, and on 4 March the last of the Chipewyan kept at York Fort was also dead. Knight was driven deeper into

Sauvage de la Baye de hudson

European artist's depiction of an Inuk drawn in his own image.

despair: 'I have done what ever lay in the Power of Man & have tended ye more than if they had been my own children . . . If I could have sav'd but one he might have Satisfy'd his Country People as wee did not Murder em.' The months of misfortune had left the Governor's own health in tatters: he complained of insomnia, frequent fainting spells, gout and a fever that 'mauled me most desperately'. For the first time, he longed for his return to England.

Only with the passage of time did Knight's will return. The first sign of recovery came in the form of a reassurance addressed to Company officials lest they think his gloomy journal entries, and personal suffering, were brought on by quaffing too much dark beer in the post's cellar. 'For fear I might be Represented A Drunkard I can Declare . . . I have not Drink'd 2 Quarts of Punch . . . nor Dramm of Brandy nor so much as a glass of Wine for above these 12 Months,' Knight swore. At the risk of appearing to protest too loudly, he addressed a similar defence to the factor at Albany Fort, 'so that no Man can brann me a Drunken Governr'. Soon he was again brooding over distant treasure.

As it turned out, the Governor faced more immediate concerns. Severe cold and food shortages had claimed many of the area's Indians and the survivors blamed the peace treaty. 'They are of the opinion the Devill must have so many Every Year & if they can but kill their Enemys they be Spar'd,' Knight fretted. By May a gang of hostile young Cree were milling around within sight of the factory, but they refused all invitations to pay it a visit. 'The very Looks of them would hang 'em all if they were before any judge whether they were guilty or not,' mused Knight. He fired three of the fort's cannons to alert those of his men who were off on a hunt, barred the gates and set a watch. When the Indian leader finally came to the factory he was wooed with offerings and the promise of a feast. Knight then issued a stern warning that if the Cree went to war with the Chipewyan he would stop all trade with them. The Governor ended his intercession by appealing to their masculinity, pointing out that they had 'Smoked the friendly Pipes and was not true men if they broke that agreement'.

The crisis averted, there came word of the return of 'Captain' Swan, one of his Indian emissaries. Knight was filled with hope, for Swan had been sent to make entreaties for peace among those who lived by the western sea. When the Indian reached York Fort to brief the anxious Governor he announced that he had been successful and had 'feasted Sung Danced & Smoked' with the distant tribe. However, the rest of Swan's tale only compounded Knight's frustration. One of the coastal Indians had travelled back with him, but after three months of trekking, had turned for home. Swan admitted that he had not actually seen the western sea, but had been assured it was near by and was convinced there would come a great trade from those parts. There was no mention of the 'Yellow Mettle' Knight so coveted.

After more than two years at York Fort, Knight could now see that his last hope of building the trade in minerals would be made through the re-establishment of a fort to the north-west, at the estuary of the Churchill River, where a Company post had been erected in 1689 only to be destroyed by fire within months. An advance party was sent ahead, and in July 1717 Knight handed over York Fort to Henry Kelsey and himself embarked for the Churchill River. On arriving there three days later, Knight suffered a further blow to his plans. Evidence had been found that a large group of Northern Indians had indeed made the great journey to the Churchill, according to his instructions, but failing to find the promised post, had left just days before the arrival of the advance party.

Shrugging off this set-back, Governor Knight stepped ashore to survey his new domain and was hotly pursued up the beach by a swarm of bloodthirsty mosquitoes. He caught a fleeting glimpse of the site where the Danish explorer Jens Munk had endured his tragic winter in 1619–20, then visited the charred ruins of the Company's abortive 1689 settlement attempt. 'I beleive they was so Discouraged that they sett it a fire to Run away by the light of it,' he later said morosely from the relative safety of his hastily erected tent. Days later the pests had found a way into the tent itself, forcing Knight to try to smoke them out. The Governor succeeded only in forcing himself through the flaps, having 'allmost Smokd my Eyes out'. The insects' voracious appetite made life especially intolerable for the men who laboured feverishly to erect the new fort before winter's onslaught. A 1952 study of northern biting flies provides support for Knight's claim that the rabid mosquitoes threatened to 'murder all the men', concluding that during an intensive attack a person would receive 280 mosquito bites on the forearm during a one-minute exposure. Further calculations demonstrated that a naked man would receive 9250 bites per minute, draining half the total blood volume in less than two hours.

When cool weather at last rid the area of the mosquitoes, clouds of black flies of near-Biblical proportions descended on the garrison, leaving Knight temporarily unhinged:

> Here is now Such Swarms of a Small Sand flyes that wee can hardly See the Sun through them . . . they flye into our Ears, Nose, Eyes, Mouth & down our throats . . . Certainly these be ye flyes that was sent as Plagues to ye Egyptians as caus'd a Darkness over the Land & brought such blotches & boiles as broke out all over them into Sores.

But Knight had overcome far greater obstacles in his years on the Bay, and soon prepared to triumph over his disappointment by selecting Richard Norton to accompany two natives in pursuit of the Northern Indians. Norton was apprenticed to the Company in 1714 and was no more than sixteen years old when ordered to make his epic inland journey to serve notice of the work undertaken for the establishment of a fort on the Churchill River which became known as Prince of Wales's Fort. He set off in a canoe on 18 July, travelling north on the trail of the Chipewyan.

Just days after Norton's departure Knight was mortified by the appearance of Inuit in the area, and by the discovery of the remains of one of their camps, so large 'it looked like a Town'. While fretting over the safety of his emissaries, he immediately began to have the post's palisades shored up, 'that my Men may not be Exposed'. The men were exposed, but only to the elements, as Knight had selected for the building site a bleak point which had less ground than 'the Royall Exchange Stands upon', but boasted as its sole redeeming feature the ability to be defended. Four bastions commanded the defensive edifice, with the men quartered in three of them and Knight occupying the fourth. In order to keep a close eye on the trade goods, the Governor stored them under the floor of his own bedchamber.

Traditional enemies of the Indians, the Inuit were virtually unknown to European traders like Knight whose knowledge was based almost exclusively on frightening tales told by Indians and the legacy of hostility from the few encounters with early explorers. Nicholas Jérémie had speculated that they were descendants of shipwrecked Basque fishermen: 'Their language, though much corrupted, has yet a certain resemblance to Basque.' Yet Jérémie detected no evidence of a pining for the Pyrenees; just for human blood. When they killed or captured an enemy, he claimed, 'they eat them raw'. In a letter of 1716 to the Committee, Knight delivered an equally hysterical assessment. 'Them natives to the northward' were 'savage and brutelike', he wrote, passing on reports that they drank blood, 'as well as some does strong drink'. In fact, his only previous direct encounter with an Inuk had come more than sixteen years before at Albany Fort, when the Cree presented him with an unfortunate 'Usquamay girl' they had captured in a raid. The only act of barbarism to which she was a party took place after Knight's departure, when Company servants saw fit to pack her off to England as a curio.

In the face of the apparent Inuit threat, Knight had small trinkets, knives, hatchets and scrapers dangled from poles pointing to the new establishment to advertise to the Inuit that there were 'Europeans this way & had things to sell'. He attested to being ready to deal even with great numbers of Inuit. Having failed to encounter any, Norton completed a 'great Sweep' of the land, locating the object of his search and convincing some to travel back to the Churchill River, where the tattered party arrived in time for Christmas 'after having endur'd a great many Hardships'. The rigours of the journey were such that Norton's mother, Sarah, later appeared before the Committee seeking financial compensation. She was awarded a gratuity of £15 on her son's behalf. On his return to the new fort, Norton and his party found that conditions there were not much better than on the Barren Lands. Knight praised the efforts of his men who had worked harder than 'Ye Negros in ye West Indies nor the Slaves at Algier' to finish the post's construction, although one who was apparently not up to the rigours, wryly referred to as 'a Young Gentleman wch hath been bredd a Lawyer', was sent back to York Fort. Knight also had harsh words for his deputy there, Henry Kelsey, who he claimed had deceived him by reporting there would be plenty of game, fish and fowl at the Churchill.

The matter was made worse by the meagre cargo of supplies delivered by the Company's frigate that August. 'I believe they would sett a Little more value upon mens Lives,' Knight grieved, 'where they but here to see the sculls & bones of Men as lyes scatter'd from the Rivers mouth to abt 12 Mile up.' The bones belonged to crewmen from Jens Munk's ill-fated attempt to discover the Northwest Passage. In 1619 Munk braved the treacherous Hudson Strait on the orders of King Christian IV of Denmark, before being chased by ice to a winter refuge at the Churchill, where within weeks the Danes lay racked with scurvy, a debilitating disease caused by Vitamin C deficiency. Munk saw scores of his men die from the affliction, 'as if a thousand knives were thrust through them'. The air of doom lifted only briefly, in midwinter, when a beautiful sunshine inspired a sermon by the ships' stricken priest. It was to be the last sermon the padre delivered in this world. Soon Munk himself fell violently ill. Praying that God would put an end to his misery, the emaciated captain wrote a last message: 'Herewith, goodnight to all the world; and my soul into the hand of God.' Two weeks later, the ice finally broke. Of the sixty-four men who had sailed from Denmark, only three remained alive to steer the sloop home, Jens Munk among them.

Not surprisingly, Munk's hideous tale put an end to Danish interest in the elusive passage. The dark waters and unknown coasts of Hudson Bay offered little enticement for judicious men, but the fatal lesson was lost on James Knight. One century had passed, and he was now plotting to revive the same naval quest that had thwarted explorers since the time of the ancients.

Woodcut from Munk's account of his disastrous voyage, showing preparations made for wintering at the mouth of the Churchill River.

6

STRANGE MAGIC

Winter's curtain of darkness hung like a shroud over James Knight, his body weakened by a lifetime spent on the Bay, his mind burdened with weariness and cold. Now that he was in his seventies, each long night made hopes of a mystic passage seem more like a dying man's prayer. Each dawn gave new birth to deception. Then, the old man began to breath the fragile air of a northern spring.

Knight's term of office finally came to an end with the arrival of the frigate *Albany* in the summer of 1718. Captain George Berley delivered the Company's authorization to return home, along with a gift of eight dozen bottles of wine to tide him over during the lengthy voyage. Leaving the northern outpost, the *Albany* carried Knight to York Fort where, in mid-September, Henry Kelsey assumed the commission as his successor as Governor-in-Chief. No longer a Company servant, Knight took the honorary title of captain. That a serious rift had developed between the two is evident from the terse communication exchanged through intermediaries as Knight sat offshore. Kelsey was apparently kept in the dark about Knight's latest scheme for discovery, learning only 'that he had sent an Indian to the golden mines'. Kelsey sought an accounting of the supplies at the Churchill post with a view to making a requisition. Knight replied that he did not have the time, but would inform the Company himself of the post's needs. 'So that,' wrote Kelsey, 'we must trust to his life which is No Certainty.' Indeed, Knight barely survived the difficult passage home.

There was fear in London that the ship had been frozen up or cast away, but on 20 November the *Albany* appeared in the Thames with a great cargo of beaver pelts and news of Knight's illness. In its next edition, *Saturday's Post* reported that Knight, 'lies lame at Limehouse by the excessive Cold he got in his Limbs in that Country, and has not yet been able to give the Company an Account of the State of their Affairs there'. A report published a month later noted his condition had not improved: 'Captain Knight, late Governour of Hudson's Bay, has lain ill ever since his Arrival.' Still, the bedridden Knight had enough energy to accept a £50 payment from the Company on 19 December.

The renewal of hope once again ended the winter. Too much had been invested in the discovery of the cliffs of gold and copper to let them slip away now. The new El Dorado did exist, beyond the Barren Lands. It was the power of that belief, the glint of that distant lucre, that saw Knight miraculously raised from his sickbed. At a Committee meeting on 20 March 1719 Sir Bibye Lake and his board considered a letter from Knight outlining a proposal for a voyage of discovery. Soon amazed Committeemen were witness as the ancient Captain himself appeared before them to pitch for an attempt at the Northwest Passage and the oft-dreamed-of metal riches. The Royal Charter under which it was founded gave the Company an effective monopoly over any new passage, but the search was long forgotten amid the demands of the trade for furs. It was forgotten no more. While Knight was no philosopher, at a time when George Berkeley was expounding his 1709 treatise *A New Theory of Vision*, which deals with sense perception, how we see distance, size and situation, he had formulated his own application of the theory. Berkeley asserted that 'the estimate we make of the distance of objects considerably remote, is rather an act of judgment grounded on experience than of sense'. Knight may not have actually seen the Strait of Anian, or the wealth of northern minerals, but then again, considered by a different standard, he had. It was through the perceptions of the Indians that Knight 'said he knew the way to the place as well as to his bedside'.

Knight goaded the directors into establishing a special sub-committee to examine his proposals. Joseph Robson, a one-time Company servant who later became an outspoken critic of its trade monopoly, argued in his *Account of Six Years Residence in Hudson's-Bay* that Knight received no encouragement. Rather, he wrote, the Company 'slept at the edge of a frozen sea', showing no interest in exploration and exerting 'all their art and power to crush that spirit in others'. Robson contends that Knight was forced to remind the Committee of their obligation under the terms of their charter to make discoveries and extend their trade, and that only after Knight threatened to seek backing from the Crown 'and accordingly waited upon one of the secretaries of state', did the Company relent. That argument finds support in a statement made in 1735 by one of the Company's veteran supply ship commanders, Captain Christopher Middleton, who was first inspired to join the Company's service by the example of Knight's expedition, and is known to have wintered at the Churchill post as early as 1721. Middleton testified that: 'The Company were against him going; but as he was *opiniatre*, they durst not disoblige him, lest he should apply elsewhere.'

Not only was there scepticism over a scheme so at odds with the pragmatism of the Company's fur trade endeavours, but given his advanced age and frail state of health, questions were raised about Knight's own fitness for the command. At a time when life expectancy in England was under forty, the very thought of sending a septuagenarian in search of the Northwest Passage approached the absurd. Still, with Knight pressing for the expedition to sail that summer, the subcommittee was forced to act. A report of 24 April noted that several meetings had been held with Knight and progress had been made towards an agreement. Later that day the entire Committee assembled to consider the matter and within a week an agreement was struck for 'Capt James Knight to goe Upon Discovery'.

After an interlude of eighty-eight years, a voyage of exploration was to once again probe the cold waters of legend. The great age of Arctic discovery in America that began with the

67

wild hopes of Frobisher and ended with the failures of Foxe and James had left a legacy of disillusionment. Now hope had been reborn. The ignorance of Incognita, the vast unknown on the world map, was to be ended by the attainment of fantastic wealth, and it was only decent that the greatest individual beneficiary would be the man who held the secret of its passage.

Entries in Company ledgers indicate that the enterprise was a joint undertaking, funded by the Hudson's Bay Company and private investors, principally Knight himself. A reference in the Company's Grand Journal notes that Knight was required to pay £142 3s 1d, 'being his proportion of 1/8 part of The Cargoe and fitting out the Albany Frigg^{tt} and Discovery Sloop on A Discovery to the Northward in Hudsons Bay, Pursuant to his Contract with the Comp^{a}'. Knight in turn received a one-eighth share in the bounty of expected riches. While the arrangement was somewhat unusual by the standard of the Company's business dealings, Knight had long since ceased being just any Company servant, having previously won a contract that allowed for a share in the profits of any mineral discoveries made while serving as Governor. Besides, the aged adventurer would have no trouble meeting his share of the financial burden; on 12 May he demanded the Committee pay up the £250 owed to him in back salary.

The discovery expedition was provided with the sturdy *Albany*, an 80-ton frigate built by James Taylor in 1716, and the 40-ton sloop *Discovery*. The *Albany* was a veteran of two previous voyages into northern waters under Captain George Berley, and was the vessel that had carried Knight home to London in 1718. Berley had first joined the Company's service as a gunner a decade earlier, and was celebrated for his defence of Albany Fort against a French attack in 1709. According to one account of the incident, French forces under their Irish commander marched up to the fort's gate and demanded the English surrender. Berley, who was on watch, told them that the Governor was asleep but that he would fetch the keys. On hearing this, the French flocked to the gate 'as close as they could stand'. On their entry, Berley greeted them instead with a face full of grapeshot fired from two six-pounders. While the account of Berley's heroics appears to be somewhat exaggerated, it was enough to earn him command of the *Albany*, which he retained for the Knight expedition.

The tiny *Discovery*, a namesake of Henry Hudson's famous vessel, had been commissioned only months earlier from the shipbuilder Thomas Crotchett, and was on her maiden voyage. Command was entrusted to David Vaughan, a Company sloop master in the Bay until the *Eastmain* was abandoned in the ice near York Fort in September 1714. Vaughan then served under Knight at York and received his hearty endorsement in a letter that assured the Committee 'you cannot have a soberer or a brisker man'. Later, in the summer of 1718, he took a hoy north and opened a trade with the Inuit. That experience, coupled with training as a ship carpenter, made Vaughan ideally suited for the command. Besides, he had joined Knight and Berley in returning to London on the *Albany* that autumn, and doubtless much of that voyage was passed scheming over the expedition of discovery. Another selected for the voyage was Alexander Apthorp, the warehouse-keeper at York Fort during Knight's tenure, whose job was now to keep an exact tally of the vast cargo of valuable minerals to be mined. One who would not make the voyage was William Stuart, an obvious choice because of his historic overland journey and knowledge of the Northern Indians. Before Knight's return to England, Henry Kelsey had written to inform him that 'Wm Stuart Poor man' had been 'lunatick', and had to be tied to his bed on several occasions. Although he was perfectly lucid for spells, Stuart's condition continued to deteriorate and he died at York Fort on 25 October 1719.

The names of just three other expedition members are known with any certainty. Benjamin Fuller, David Newman and John Awdry were ordered to serve on board the *Albany*. It is possible to speculate on others. Company minutes refer to the payment of a gratuity to a certain Thomas Hall, whose name appears under Knight's own, separate from the officers and crews. This suggests Hall may have been engaged in a senior capacity relating to Knight's quest for minerals. Excluding the commanders, it is estimated that the *Albany* carried a crew of seventeen, while ten manned the *Discovery*, the latter figure confirmed by a notation in the minutes in reference to an application for an Admiralty protection for that number against press-gangs. Ten other 'Landsmen Passengers' – described in a newspaper report as artificers and a 'Dry Nurse', or work foreman – also joined the expedition into the unknown, bringing the total to forty.

Company records contain indents for a cargo of trading goods to be taken, including knives, scissors, muskets, awls, blankets, beads, fish hooks, waistcoat buttons and '8 squard Looking glasses'. The Company also approved the purchase of 3500 bricks and three hogsheads of lime and wood frames for building a winter shelter. Knight was well aware of the dangers of inadequate shelter from a century before, 'When the Dane Captain Monk wintered at Churchill River'. Heating would be supplied by twenty chaldrons (26 cubic metres) of coal loaded aboard the *Albany*. Provisions far exceeding those taken on routine Company trading voyages to its Hudson Bay outposts were carefully stored, among them quantities of flour, bread, butter, bacon, stock fish, beef and pork. The crew's thirst would be quenched by strong beer, brandy and spirits. The food should have been adequate for a single Arctic winter, although large quantities of salt were taken and it is clear that, as he had done at York Fort and the Churchill River, Knight intended to rely on the hunt to supplement the men's diet. Knight observed that though the Danes were a 'hardy sort of People', their graves at the Churchill testified to 'what wee must trust too if wee doo not provide before Winter Setts in'. Mrs Isabella Ellis was commissioned to sew the ships' colours, and lastly, strong-boxes were made, bound with iron, to stow the treasure.

At a Committee meeting on 22 May instructions were ordered drawn up for Berley and Vaughan directing that they 'Saile to any Place where The S^d Capt James Knight shall order Them'. For the captains, Knight's authority was absolute, the only exception being the actual navigation of their ships. In case the vessels were separated in bad weather while crossing the Atlantic, they were ordered to rendezvous at Resolution Island at the entrance to Hudson Strait. If separated beyond that point, they were to conduct their explorations independently, with Knight directing Berley in the *Albany* and with Vaughan instructed to guide the *Discovery* to:

> 64 Degrees North Latitude and from thence Northward to Endeavour to find out the Streights of Anian, and as Often as Conveniently you can to send your Boats to the Shoar side in order to find how high the Tide Rises and wht. Point of the Compas the flood comes from.

The sixty-fourth parallel, in the area of Roe's Welcome, was where Luke Foxe had detected a flood-tide from the west during his 1631 voyage aboard the *Charles*. In 1613 Thomas Button had similarly observed 'a strong race of a tyde' near the channel, which he called Ne Ultra. Such a tide provided evidence for the existence of a Northwest Passage to the Pacific, the entry point of the Strait of Anian. Knight's interest in Roe's Welcome first surfaced in a notation of 12 May 1716 in his York Journal that describes the passage as 'still one of the furthest Rivers but it lyes further to the Norward than any of our Discoverers has Discovered'. His intention is confirmed by an entry in the Committee's minute book which describes the resolve to make 'A Discovery of A NW Passage beyond Tho' Buttons'. In the fashion of the first Northwest Passage expeditions, whose hopes of skirting America were driven by the vision of Oriental riches, Knight's own orders make it clear that any triumph in the discovery of the passage would simply be a means to a lucrative end. The intended voyage would 'by Gods Permission . . . find out the Streight of Annian', Knight was told, 'by Order to Discover Gold and Other Valuable Comodities to the Northward'. In the unhappy event of failure, he was to 'Husband Everything to the best Advantage', which meant attempting to recoup some of the expenses through enhanced trade and the establishment of a whale fishery.

Knight's use of the term 'Strait of Anian' for what was widely referred to among English explorers as the Northwest Passage is curious. Professor Glyndwr Williams has raised the possibility that Knight had studied one or more of the French and Dutch maps of the early eighteenth century, such as the *Globe Terrestre* published in 1708 by the French geographer J.B. Nolin, which placed the eastern entrance to the Strait of Anian at the north-west coast of Hudson Bay. It is possible Knight encountered these charts while in Holland in 1710 for the months of peace negotiations which led to the signing of the Treaty of Utrecht. In his treatise *The British Search for the Northwest Passage in the Eighteenth Century*, Williams argues that 'such maps would be treated with more than usual attention at this time because of the long French occupation of York Fort'.

Knight's advanced age resulted in special instructions to be opened only in the event of his death. They specified the two captains were to continue the attempt to 'Obtain all sorts of Trade & Commerce . . . Especially to find out the Gold and Copper Mines', using directions left behind by Knight. The secrecy that surrounded Knight's intentions is apparent from the exclusion of his detailed written directions from the sailing orders and instructions issued to Berley and Vaughan while in London. Likewise the commanders were ordered not only to deliver up their own journals and those belonging to their mates, but all other journals kept on board their respective vessels 'if you Can Discover Any'. After obtaining the best possible cargo, the *Albany* and the *Discovery* were further commanded to make directly for the Port of London without visiting any other port or place, 'But in Case of your utmost Extremity and not to Break Bulk'.

One ominous clause in the commander's instructions was to address the growing dispute that had arisen between the ex-governor and his former deputy. On his return to London, Knight had levelled serious charges at Henry Kelsey over his alleged complicity with Indians who had made off with 'several Bundles out of the Trading Roome in the Night'. Kelsey was informed of both the allegations and the identity of his accuser in a letter of 1719 from the Committee, which also demanded a detailed response. In the meantime, the discovery expedition was ordered to steer clear of Kelsey and all of the Company's posts, bound by instructions that went to lengths to ensure that the ships would call at the Churchill River port, York Fort or

Albany Fort only 'in Case of the Utmost Extremity only to Preserve yᵉ Shipp, Sloop & Mens Lives', and on such an occasion
the expedition would 'be Absolutely Under the Direction' of
Kelsey, apparently to avoid further conflict between the two
factions. Knight was further warned that if he should encounter
Kelsey or any of his officers, he must show them 'all Possible
Respect and Neither Molest or Hinder them'.

Kelsey was predictably bitter on learning of the charges,
fuming 'I am very sure they have done all the prejudice lies
in their Power by fals asspersions.' He further professed a
hearty desire that the Company would not suffer any great
losses 'by yᵉ Discoverers'. Kelsey attributed 'the efects of
their Mallice to turn me out of my Employ for no other
reason then their being afraid of being out done'. Kelsey
had his own, somewhat less imaginative plan for expand-
ing the Company's trade through discovery to the north.
Before learning of Knight's expedition he had taken a sloop
on a short jaunt up the north-west coast of Hudson Bay
with promising results. 'I saw many Esquemoes and gott
some whalebone Oyle and Some Sea Horse teeth,' wrote
Kelsey.

It was on 2 June 1719 that Sir Bibye Lake and his Committee adjourned to Gravesend to oversee final preparations for
the first expedition of discovery to sail from English shores
in search of a Northwest Passage in close to a century. If
not a hoard of golden treasure, they hoped at least to
recoup their investments, but for Captain James Knight the
voyage marked not just a chance of riches, but the wealth
of peace that comes after a lifetime of struggle. On the eve
of their departure on 5 June a reception was held for Knight
and the ships' captains, and the Committee paid the men's
wages, presented them each with a guinea for drink and the
officers with a gratuity for fresh provisions, before wishing
the aged discoverer a prosperous voyage and a safe return.
With an ironic reference to the 'Strange magick Power of
Gold', *Saturday's Post* trumpeted to its readers that 'Captain
Knight imbarked on board a Ship in the River for the North
Pole, in order to make a Discovery of a Gold Mine in Terra

Borealis'. Knight took his crudely drawn Indian maps, his explorers' narratives and his misplaced dreams, and directed the *Albany* and the *Discovery* towards the limits of the known world.

7

DEAD MAN'S ISLAND

There was no relief. No consolation. Only the silence of an Arctic tomb. Steering the route that Hudson's Bay Company frigates had plied for half a century, the *Albany* and the *Discovery* soon pointed their bowsprits westward into the unknown, and vanished utterly. For two years Knight's benefactors awaited word of his discoveries, but none came. Finally, voice was given to the unspoken fears that something had gone horribly wrong. 'Wee Cannot but Admire what is become of Capt. Knight, not haveing heard any thing from him to this time,' the Governor and Committee wrote to Henry Kelsey on 26 May 1721. By the time he had received the letter, Kelsey already knew the terrible answer.

The explorers spent their first winter on the north-west coast of Hudson Bay, 'in about 62^d 30^m odd', the area of Marble Island. That news had come from John Hancock, master of the *Prosperous*, who was sent north from York Fort in 1720 to carry on the trade in whale oil and walrus tusks Kelsey had begun the previous year. Hancock was told of the expedition's whereabouts by area Inuit, although no mention was made that the crews were in distress. Kelsey, still fuming over Knight's charges against him, observed snidely that 'the goldfinders winter'd where wee had been last Summer and had traded with those Indians and Spoiled our Trade'. Kelsey responded by developing a competing 'designe of Wintering to the Northward', which was rejected by the Committee in a letter the following year that set out in no uncertain terms his inability to prepare and provide adequately for such an undertaking: 'wee cannot Aprove of your Wintering further Northward to the Hazard of yr Life'. Kelsey was advised to limit his northern search for trade to the summer months.

On 16 April 1721 the factor Richard Staunton, who had succeeded Knight at the new fort on the Churchill River (which Knight had requested the Committee name and was so designated Prince of Wales's Fort) received a curious report from a large party of Northern Indians. They informed Staunton that the more distant Copper Indians had encountered white men the previous summer, and that 'thay had seen som of our Country men & y^t thay had given them a great Deale of Iron'. This evocative intelligence was soon superseded by more ominous news. During his sloop journey north months later, Kelsey discovered the first evidence of disaster, items from the missing expedition found in the possession of the Inuit. The possibility that tragedy had overtaken the expedition's forty men does not appear to have fazed him in the least. Kelsey was moved neither to act nor to pity, simply recording in his personal journal on 9 August: 'I bore away because ye winds did not favour my Intentions of going farther to ye N^{o}ward to look for ye place where ye albany sloop was lost we seeing things belonging to those vessels.'

It was the prevailing wisdom of the Company that, for safety's sake, the trading hoys must return from the north no later than the end of August or beginning of September. Kelsey was back at the Churchill on 16 August, belying any claims of a resolve to undertake an immediate search. Faced with the possibility that expedition survivors could have been saved, he did what everyone else would not have done. Kelsey's failure to launch a rescue attempt the following year only casts further doubt on his motives. In a letter to another Company servant, an embittered Kelsey argued that Knight's allegations, 'represented so Odiously to Our Masters', had damaged his reputation, 'wch is more Valuable yn Life itselfe'. Whether by malice or negligence, Kelsey had his revenge.

When the sloop *Whalebone* was sent from the Churchill in 1722, it was to sail along the north-west coast of Hudson Bay in an attempt to locate copper mines. To that end Richard

Norton, Knight's former apprentice, joined the crew. Yet nowhere in Kelsey's instructions to Master John Scroggs is there an order to search for the missing ships, the only reference being a postscript identifying the place where Knight was reported to have wintered. Compounding the problem was the character of Scroggs himself, an indifferent navigator, judged by contemporaries to be 'a timerous person, and no Way fond of the Expedition', whose observations were criticized by subsequent explorers of the Bay's north-west coast. It was by sheer accident that Scroggs came across artefacts belonging to the *Albany* and the *Discovery*. On his outward voyage, Scroggs, 'in the Latitude of 62 Deg. 48 Min. sent a Boat for a peice of Wood, which was a-float, and they found it to be the lower Part of the Ships Foremast, broke off about five Foot above the Deck'. The relic lay in the choppy waters off the coast of Marble Island, then still known as Brooke Cobham.

The sloop continued north, mistaking Chesterfield Inlet for a western passage, but rather than pursue this possible opening to the Pacific, Scroggs chose to turn back. On his return journey he tacked along the coast of Marble Island, naming its prominent geographical feature, the island's high point, Pits Mount. Anchoring off the island, Scroggs sent a boat ashore to search for further wreckage from the missing vessels. Soon Scroggs was hurrying back to the Churchill with news of a startling discovery. He had been 'where the Albany and Discovery Sloop where both Ship-wracked'.

Unfortunately the log of the *Whalebone*, with its vital clues, has been lost. Instead there are only tantalizing second-hand references to what Scroggs had seen on the barren isle. On 25 July 1722 Richard Staunton recorded in his journal that Scroggs 'doth Affirm that Every Man was Killed by the Eskemoes, wch I am heartily Sorry for their hard fortune'. The very next day Scroggs provided Staunton with further assurance 'that them that went upon the Discovery to the Norw^d all perished'. His conclusion that the Knight expedition crews had been attacked and killed by the Inuit may have been based solely on circumstantial evidence. Excerpts derived from Scroggs's missing log appeared in later accounts of the geography of the region, revealing that the master had stumbled upon an Inuit camp on Marble Island where ships' spars had been 'split into Tent Poles, and Tents covered with Sails'. The evidence for Knight's destruction was everywhere. A medicine chest, ice-poles, cabin lining and part of a mast were found in the possession of the natives. Scroggs tried to trade iron but the Inuit were not interested, which suggests that they had scavenged a supply of the metal from the missing vessels. An account of the master's journal published twenty-six years later does expand on his theory of the Knight expedition's destruction, recording: 'Scroggs thought that some of them were drowned, and that others had suffered in a Fray with the Eskemaux.' Then came evidence for what Scroggs took to be the frightening confirmation of an Inuit attack; the appearance of an Inuk man bearing 'a large Scar on his Cheek, like a Cut with a Cutlass, and at that time a green Wound'.

Nothing remained of Captain James Knight's golden dreams but paperwork for the Company's London bureaucrats. Recalled by the Committee, Henry Kelsey brought confirmation of the expedition's destruction to London in the autumn of 1722. But even a month before Kelsey's arrival, on 29 September, apparently on the strength of the Kelsey's conclusion made a year earlier that the vessels were 'lost', the *Albany* and the *Discovery* were written off the Company's books, having been 'Castaway to the Northward In Hudsons Bay on A Discovery anno 1720'. This action was taken without any effort to confirm the report or mount a search for survivors, or even to reclaim some of its estimated investment of £7–8000. For the first time in the 250-year search for a Northwest Passage, a discovery expedition had been utterly destroyed. Not a single man aboard ever returned. Captain James Knight, after having spent twenty years of his life on Hudson Bay, had become the first expedition commander to die in the region since Henry Hudson. In the end there was no glittering splendour of riches, only brutal suffering, and when life outlasted hope, a death grimly aware of failure.

While Kelsey's cruel indifference towards the expedition's fate is best viewed in light of his feud with Knight, it was later seen as part of a grand design to thwart discovery of the North-west Passage. In his critique of Company affairs Joseph Robson condemned the London Committee for failing to order Kelsey to undertake a search: 'poor Knight . . . he was not worth their care . . . such cruel negligence is not very reconcileable with an approbation of his voyage'. Robson argued that the Hudson's Bay Company never supported the venture, nor any serious attempt at finding a Northwest Passage, because the discovery of such a passage would have threatened its own monopoly on northern trade. 'They did not value the loss of the ship and sloop as long as they were rid of those troublesome men,' he concluded. Robson was certainly a prejudiced observer, yet the indifference with which the Company received the news of the expedition's destruction lends credence to his allegations.

While it ranks as the greatest mystery of Arctic exploration, the disaster stirred none of the popular interest that later characterized the destruction of Sir John Franklin's 1845 expedition. There were no memorials of Carrara marble, or teary odes to the fallen explorer, 'and thou Heroic Sailor Soul!'. No Royal Navy relief expeditions launched or parliamentary rewards established. It was viewed simply as the fulfilment of one man's folly. Innuendo about Knight's doomed quest for the Strait of Anian would seem to be found even in *Gulliver's Travels*. First published in 1726, Jonathan Swift's classic satire places Brobdingnag, the imaginary land of giants, at precisely the place of Knight's expected land of 'Yellow Mettle'. Early editions of *Gulliver's Travels* even contain maps siting Brobdingnag on the west coast of America, and showing the elusive Strait of Anian nearby.

Knight's will was finally executed in September 1724, and contains the only surviving reference to his private life and family. His 'Loving Wife Elizabeth' received the bulk of the estate and his son Gilpin just one shilling, 'he having been already advanced by me in the world Considerably more than my Circumstances'. With Knight's death, the charges against Kelsey were quietly dropped, although the one-time boy explorer who became Governor-in-Chief was never allowed to return to duty in Hudson Bay. Kelsey petitioned the Company in 1724 to allow him to command a voyage into the Bay, but the offer was rejected. Four years earlier Kelsey had sworn of Knight and his allies that 'if it please God I live to see ym shall Endeavour to make ym prove their Asertion'. His own actions precluded such a hearing ever being held. Kelsey died that autumn, the remarkable overland treks of his youth long forgotten, his subsequent service clouded by the allegations and suspicion that had characterized his final years.

After Scroggs's discoveries confirmed the Knight disaster, Company trading sloops steered clear of the perilous northwest coast of Hudson Bay. It was not until fifteen years later that the Hudson's Bay Company ordered another attempt to locate the Northwest Passage, and then only after the wealthy Irish zealot Arthur Dobbs had severely criticized the Company and vigorously campaigned for a revival of the search. Dobbs, Surveyor-General of Ireland and a member of the Irish parliament who later served as Governor of North Carolina, presented the apocryphal 1592 voyage of Juan de Fuca as evidence for the existence for the passage. Later, Dobbs also cited the account of an imaginary voyage made by one Bartholomew De Fonte, purportedly a Spanish admiral, who claimed to have sailed north from Lima in 1640 and traversed the Northwest Passage. During the voyage through what he called the 'Sea of Ronquillo', the Spaniard maintained that he had encountered a Boston trader captained by a man called Shapley. Dobbs became convinced that Shapley was engaged in the fur trade and that the passage was located in Hudson Bay. Armed with further evidence of flood-tides on the west coast of the Bay encountered by Button and Foxe, Dobbs pressed for a resumption of exploration.

His initial attempts were rebuffed, but Dobbs persisted, dogging Hudson's Bay Company Deputy Governor Samuel Jones around London in 1733. Jones, who had served on the subcommittee which had negotiated with Knight, finally agreed to a meeting, discouraging Dobbs by recounting the disappearance of Knight's two ships, 'telling me of the great Expense and Loss they had been'. Jones's story included the discovery by

Scroggs of 'a Piece of the Ship's Stern', and ended with the gloomy conclusion that the expedition was 'lost or surpriz'd by the Natives, and the Ships broke up'. Instead of putting Dobbs off, the account of the Knight disaster only served to pique his interest and he asked to see Scroggs's journal. Jones then made the amazing claim that Scroggs had kept no log. In fact, extracts of the valuable document later surfaced, although the mysterious subsequent disappearance of the original journal from the Company's archives has never been explained. Dobbs left the meeting more determined than ever:

> for any Thing they knew, [Knight's] Ships might have made their Passage, or at least one of them, and by some Accident might have been afterwards lost; and the Wreck they saw might as well be after the Ship's Return, as before they got into the Passage: For if they had been lost in the Bay, it was probable some of them might have reach'd Churchill Factory.

A decade later Dobbs changed his tune, conceding that if Knight's crews had not succeeded in making the passage, they were 'probably in the Winter surprized by the Natives'. This revised theory was apparently based on intelligence gathered from Company traders who had observed that natives living in the area where the expedition was lost, 'are shyer since that Time in trading with the Company's Sloops, which they apprehend to be from a Consciousness of Guilt'.

In an effort to appease Dobbs, the Company finally sent an expedition north from Churchill in 1737, but it crept only as far as Whale Cove before turning back, 'the coast being so perrilous'. Furious at the feeble attempt, Dobbs enlisted the aid of the senior Company commander, Captain Christopher Middleton, who, inspired by Knight's undertaking, had first signed on with the Company in 1721 in the hope of joining a voyage of discovery. A skilled navigator, Middleton was scheduled to sail with Scroggs the year Knight relics were discovered on Marble Island, but the less able Scroggs refused to take him. Middleton was well aware at the time of the

Company's reluctance to outfit even Knight for the purpose of discovery. Now, together with Dobbs, he took to hounding the British Admiralty to join the search for the Northwest Passage.

Even the formidable Royal Navy could muster no defence against the persistent Dobbs. The result was that Middleton was granted command of HMS *Furnace*, with William Moor commanding HMS *Discovery*, in what was the Royal Navy's first attempt at the Northwest Passage. In 1742 Middleton's expedition sailed into the unknown waters of Roe's Welcome, probing Wager Bay and Repulse Bay and reaching the entrance of Frozen Strait, before conceding defeat. On its return voyage, the expedition stopped at Brooke Cobham. Not realizing the island was that charted by Luke Foxe in 1631, members of Middleton's expedition renamed it Marble Island after the appearance of the quartzite. A boat was sent ashore for fresh water, and in an entry of 14 August 1742 in his *Discovery* journal, Moor confirmed the existence of 'a great Deal of the Wreck of Capt Barlows [Berley's] Ship and Sloop, which were Supposed to be Lost near this Latit'. John Rankin, lieutenant aboard the *Furnace*, discovered a harbour at the west end of the island and took soundings there. Observations of the tides at Marble Island also convinced Rankin of the 'great Probability' that on the mainland near by, a passage, or straits, 'leading to some western Ocean' would be found. Middleton decided otherwise, and the ships soon departed.

Soon after returning to London, Middleton was challenged by Dobbs, who attacked the captain for not following up the lead. Middleton's case was further weakened when several officers, including Moor and Rankin, alleged that he had been paid off by the Company. Dobbs was more interested in challenging the Hudson's Bay Company's trading monopoly than finding the passage, although it was the latter consideration that was kept at the forefront of public attention. It was, as Middleton put it, the 'cloak to cover other designs'. Dobbs successfully orchestrated a drive for the establishment of a £20,000 Parliamentary prize for discovery of the Northwest Passage, and then set off in pursuit of it, creating the private North West Committee to raise funds for an expedition under Moor, who was given command of the *Dobbs Galley*. A second vessel, the *California*, was to sail under Captain Francis Smith, a veteran commander of several Hudson's Bay Company trading voyages from Churchill River to Whale Cove.

Perhaps inspired by the example of their mentor, incessant backbiting between Moor and Smith doomed whatever hopes they had of discovering conclusive evidence for the existence of a passage. The undertaking's main geographic accomplishment, the partial exploration of Chesterfield Inlet, added little to what had previously been learned by Middleton. Where they did succeed was to add further insight into the fate of the Knight expedition. In August 1746 the ships anchored off Marble Island to check the tides, while hunting parties were sent ashore. Intrigued by the island's unsual appearance, Dobbs's agent, Henry Ellis, explored the 'rent and shattered' landscape, reporting the discovery among the rubble of deep caverns where 'one may hear a great

These are all Fathoms.

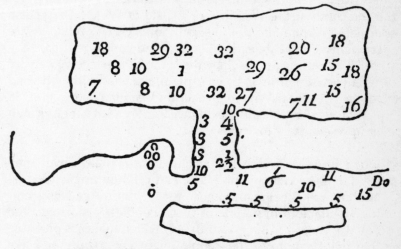

This lyeth off the Mouth of the Cove.

Map recording Lieutenant Rankin's soundings taken at the west harbour, Marble Island.

Noise, as of considerable Streams rolling over Rocks'. Some of the groundwater oozed out of cliffs, staining the white rock brilliant green and convincing Ellis of the existence of 'copper, or other Mines'. There were everywhere eerie 'tracts of the Eskimaux', including stands of stone, *inuksuit*, which Ellis attributed to 'some superstitious Custom', and the burial chambers of their dead.

Engaged in the more menial pursuit of collecting driftwood for a fire, the hunters stumbled on the stave of a buoy and a piece of oak, 'with such Trunnel Holes as are made in Ships Sides'. In his *Account of a Voyage For the Discovery of a North-West Passage*, Theodore Swaine Drage, the clerk of the *California*, concluded, 'in all probability they were Part of the Remains of the Wreck of the Ships in which Mr Knight, and Mr Barlow [*sic*] were lost'. Drage had no doubt that the shoals and rocks of the area's coarse coastline had served as the ships' graveyard. 'There are few Coasts in the World, upon which an Accident of this Kind could be sooner expected,' he observed, adding that Knight's vessels had probably been 'set a Ground, or on the Shoals, or Rocks, either from the Darkness of the Night, the thickness of the Weather, or a Gale of Wind'. Drage also speculated on the fate of the expedition's crews. While aware that twenty-five years earlier Scroggs had concluded that they were killed during an attack by the Inuit, Drage received a very different account from his own captain. Francis Smith, who had made six voyages to Whale Cove for the Company between 1738 and 1744, revealed startling evidence that some of Knight's men may have survived for years:

> when he traded with the Eskemaux at Whale Cove, they used to shew him a young Lad, and call him English Mane, alluding to his being an English Man, whose Age was seemingly suitable to the Time of these Peoples Misfortune, the Lad appeared as of a mixed Breed, which makes it probable that one or more of the People might get Ashore and live sometime amongst the Eskemaux.

With the severe gusts of winter already coming on, and faced with the tragic lesson of Knight's destruction, Smith and Moor soon bore away for more temperate climes. It was a decade before the quest was again taken up, this time with the *Argo* sailing from Philadelphia on an unsuccessful American attempt at the Northwest Passage, underwritten by no less a light than Benjamin Franklin.

Dobbs's agitation reached its logical conclusion in 1749 when his efforts forced Parliamentary hearings to be held into the Hudson's Bay Company's monopoly. Influenced in part by exaggerated claims by the Company of an enviable record of exploration in which the search for the Northwest Passage figured prominently, the committee of the House of Commons found in its favour. This might have been viewed as a confirmation of a long-standing Company policy of obsessive secrecy over its operations, except that it was this very secretiveness which had inspired much of the criticism in the first place. One writer went so far as to censure the Company for inciting the belief that Hudson Bay was 'the most forlorn and dreadful Part of the Universe'. Surely, had the hardship and dangers encountered by the Company and its employees in the conduct of their business in such a climate been better known, such an assessment would rather have been readily accepted. With his stated goal of 'doing Good, by making Discoveries of the Great World' finally thwarted, Dobbs devoted himself to his apiary, finding some comfort in the company of the 'inhabitants of the Little World; particularly that most useful and industrious Society of Bees'. He did, however, keep one hand in the honey jar, with sporadic attacks on the Hudson's Bay Company. Three years later he was appointed Governor of North Carolina.

It was not until 1765 that further accounts appeared about the expedition's fate. Moses Norton, chief factor at Prince of Wales's Fort – by this time a huge stone fortress that had in 1731 replaced Knight's wooden trading post at the Churchill River – had overseen a succession of whaling and trade voyages along the Bay's north-west coast. Later accused by one of his subordinates, Samuel Hearne, of being a polygamist and notorious smuggler who lived 'in open defiance of every law, human and divine', Norton is nonetheless credited with learning grim details of the Knight tragedy from two Inuit boys obtained during one of the voyages.

The first boy, a thirteen-year-old, was purchased at Cape Esquimaux in July 1765 by the Company sloop master Magnus Johnston for a sword and other trade goods. Johnston reported that the lad's father was so happy with his share of the haul that he let out 'Hedious yeals' of joy. Apparently the boy's mother was not so enamoured with the arrangement, for the man skulked back to the sloop two days later to ask for his son's return. Johnston, convinced the boy he had purchased could be made a tool 'to Ingratiate the Esquimaux towards us or any other Christian people', flatly refused. The man then offered up a second son, explaining that 'he would lett his brother go with him to keep him company'. When Johnston returned to Prince of Wales's Fort, he handed Norton an 'Exacte Account of the Esquimaux Trade' he had obtained on the voyage: 'Wolves – 5, White Foxes – 4, Wolveren – 1, Esquimax Boys – 2'.

Norton had a particular interest in the fate of the Knight

Arthur Dobbs.

expedition. His father, Richard, was the apprentice sent into the Barrens by Knight in 1717, and had later seen evidence of the expedition's destruction while serving under Scroggs. With the aid of an interpreter, the chief factor asked the two boys if they knew anything of the disaster. Repeating stories told by their elders, they confirmed that two vessels had been lost at Marble Island in the autumn, but that the crews made it safely ashore, where they had constructed 'Huts wth moss and clay'. Using iron salvaged from the wrecks, the crews traded for bear flesh and whale and seal blubber with Inuit inhabiting the island. Yet without proper food and clothing, their numbers quickly dwindled 'so that none of them Survived ye Winter'.

Norton gained new information about the site of the disaster and the fate of the missing vessels, describing it as 'near Marble Harbour where those unhappy People had their huts'. As for the ships, 'What Mr Richard Norton & Mr Scrogs saw of ye wracks in ye year 1722 was but ye Least part of it', the bulk of the wreckage having been taken up by the natives. The boys' account had a chilling conclusion. Marble Island, they said, was now haunted by the dead. 'Ever since that misfortune ye Esquimay has not Inhabited on Marble Island as they call it ye Dead Mans Island by so many Englishmen Perishing on it,' Norton scrawled in his post journal on 29 November 1765. 'They say that Even themselves Died faster then usual while they was upon it & for this Reason they Dont chuse to Rendevouse there.'

Questioning the accuracy of the boys' account, Norton suggested that at least some of the expedition survivors might have indeed been destroyed by the Inuit as Scroggs had reported forty-three years earlier. 'But I have ye Vanity to think that if any accident was to Hapen to an English vessels now . . . that ye Natives as far north as Marble Island would Rather assist a man in Distress,' he added. To that end he had the boys, 'Clothed in English Riggin & likewise In a good state of health', returned to their father the following summer. Norton's faith in the northerners was in stark contrast to recent experience. When the *Dobbs Galley* and *California* visited Marble Island in 1746, the vessels sat offshore for some time before sending armed parties ashore, and even then they were ordered 'not to ramble far from the Boats and to keep together that they might not be surprised'. As late as 1750, when the sloop master James Walker began to make annual trading runs from Prince of Wales's Fort north to Whale Cove, on the mainland south of Marble Island, he was specifically warned against possible Inuit attack.

On his maiden voyage Walker found the Inuit at Whale Cove to be 'Impertinent and savvy', and complained they had threatened to kill Indian hunters taken along for the voyage. During his 1753 stop Walker was attacked and stabbed aboard his sloop by a native wielding an ice chisel. The injured master forced the culprit off his vessel at pistol point. The next day a throng of Inuit gathered on nearby rocks and began to sharpen their iron-tipped lances and make threatening gestures. Walker had the sloop's moorings cut in order to make an escape, but just as the vessel got under sail it was surrounded by armed men in kayaks. On the shore another one hundred and fifty

An Inuk in his kayak.

natives prepared to join the attempt to seize the sloop. Walker and his tiny crew only narrowly escaped. It took a decade of uneventful trading voyages along the north-west coast to finally allay fears of Inuit hostility. Only then did Company vessels again return to the haunted ground of Marble Island.

There is no first-person account of that dramatic moment in July 1767 when the harpooners from the sloop *Success* unwittingly discovered the final refuge of the Knight expedition. There is only the journal of Master Joseph Stevens, who travelled the next day to investigate the discovery of 'The Ruins of ye House'. Stevens instructed his men 'to separate a bought ye Rockes & harbour as much as possible and to let me know what they did see'. The value of their survey is measured in the tremendous level of detail in which Stevens recorded the discoveries of relics from the mysterious expedition. Together with the log of Magnus Johnston of the *Churchill*, who visited the site ten days later, they provide the most precise record of the aftermath of disaster.

In his 23 July entry in the *Success* journal, Stevens compiled meticulous descriptions of, alternately, the ruin, coal pile, anchors, wood, shoes and whalebone. The measurements of the ruined shelter, taken from the interior, were listed as '47 feet from inside to inside and Breadth 29 feet'. The foundation walls were of stone, mud and moss, 'raised from ye Surface of ye Earth . . . ab^t 5 feet high'. Inside and about the ruin were four to five hundred bricks, many of which appeared freshly made. Everywhere were signs that the Inuit had made extensive use of the expedition materials. Stevens noted that while the natives had left the scattered heap of 'very good burning Coal' untouched, the wooden features of the shelter had been removed for fuel. Johnston later added that 'It has bene a Woodn frem to the Howse – and its very plain to be seen, Now every hole where the posts stood, which is all Dugg out and gone By the Esquimaux.' Similarly, at the place judged to be where carpenters had set up shop, 'by ye quantity of chipes there which are in general New England Oake', some of the timbers were fashioned in such a way as to 'be ye Natives works'.

Among the wood Stevens found pieces of a ship's carved work, side steps and part of the channel-wale, leading him to conclude the ship had been not less than 140 tons, and that there was 'Many Reason to Judge of her being lost as it has been Ships Timbers ye Carpenters were at work on'. Shanks of three anchors were also found, with the stems broken off at the palms and the rings removed. Stevens was uncertain whether the damage had been done by the Inuit or expedition members. Two of the anchors 'seemes to have been a Long Time there by there being much rust', although the third 'has less appearance of age then anyone I have belonging to ye Success'. Difference in size caused additional confusion, leaving Stevens to believe 'there has been more then one vessel there and at Different times'. One intriguing clue used to support that theory was provided by footwear found at the site, which Stevens decided had the appearance of French fashion and workmanship, and concluded belonged to officers. One heel, though, was attributed to 'some common hands' from the large pegs and the coarseness of the work. From this, he argued, 'my opinion is that ye French has Wintered there is a smaller vessell and has gone well off'.

The whalers were frustrated by their failure to 'find any thing remarkable, such as papers'. So far, the only bone seen was not human, but a great many pieces of whalebone, including a large crown. Days later Stevens returned to the site, this time armed with hatchets and shovels and accompanied by Johnston, who was curious to see 'where those Unfortenet people has ben lost'. According to Stevens, 'we Dug in ye Ruins of ye House ab^t 3 feet down & find ye flore to be laid in a Workman like manner wth Brick & Mortor we also found there a scull whether Native or Christian is not to say'. Johnston describes the discovery as being 'severall English mens shoes & a Humen Skull – Some of our people Tok it to be a Womans skull'. The only evidence of writing remained that found earlier on the shank of an anchor, and it meant nothing: 'E S 5. 166'. It was left to Samuel Hearne, the young mate of the *Churchill*, to confirm the extent of the horror that had been uncovered.

On the eve of embarking at Prince of Wales's Fort for the

voyage that took him to Marble Island, Hearne had wandered away from the stone battlements to a place near the Churchill River, where he scratched his name on the face of a boulder for posterity: 'Sl. Hearne, July 1, 1767'. He was just twenty-two, had only recently joined the Hudson's Bay Company, but had already spent a decade at sea, commencing as a captain's servant in the Royal Navy during the Seven Years War. Hearne's confident gesture foretold his destiny: to become, before his thirtieth birthday, one of the greatest figures in the history of northern exploration. But at Marble Island, three years before he would embark on his own search for the elusive copper mines and Northwest Passage, using crude navigational instruments and Indian guides in a remarkable journey across a barren wilderness of 360,000 square kilometres, Hearne saw firsthand the ghastly face of discovery's failure.

There are differing accounts of precisely what Hearne encountered when he returned to the desolate cove on 6 August to collect coal. The logbooks of both Johnston and Stevens mention his discovery, in the midst of a fierce lightning storm, of many graves. In Johnston's words, 'they had found A great Number of graves one of which Mr Hearne cawsed the people to Digg up in order to sea if they find Any thing Remarkable – but could not – only the Bons of a Stout man who without Doubt is one of the Unhappey Sufferars'. Stevens recorded that 'on their diging up part of a soft raising ground they found ye sculls & bones of Differant humane Bodies'. Curiously, in his own narrative, published years later, Hearne recounted seeing various articles during his visits to the disaster site that summer, among them anchors, cables and bricks, 'which the hand of time had not defaced', yet he makes no mention of a graveyard. When the sloops finally sailed for Prince of Wales's Fort, the true origin of the victims remained a mystery, and despite all that had been seen, the whalers remained unsure of the source of their suffering. In Johnston's words, 'wither they was Starv'd with could or hunger or Destroyd by the Natives is a thing I cannot find out As yet'.

The next year Stevens returned to Marble Island with the *Success* now in company with the shallop *Speedwell*, commanded by Hearne. On 3 August 1768 Stevens ordered three whale boats and their crews to the harbour at the eastern end which would serve as a base for the whale hunt. Six days later Stevens and Hearne went to the harbour and received the disappointing news that 'there was but a Poor show of Fish this season'. The commanders did not leave the site empty-handed, though. Stevens recorded the discovery of another relic of the mysterious shipwreck found the previous year, a ship's figurehead: 'We found one of ye Vessels Heads that was lost there: it is a man head and I have it on board.' In the log of the *Speedwell* Hearne made no mention of the discovery.

In 1769 the whalers again converged on Marble Island. Stevens was now master of the brig *Charlotte*, with Hearne serving as mate, and once again they had a rendezvous with Magnus Johnston in the *Churchill*. By then, the relics had finally

Samuel Hearne.

92

been identified as belonging to Knight's lost ships. On another visit to the disaster site Hearne encountered several aged Inuit and, through a Company linguist, interrogated them at length. Hearne characterized the account they received as being 'full, clear, and unreserved'. Incredibly, although Johnston had questioned the Inuit two years earlier and had been unsuccessful in learning the cause of the disaster, Hearne now returned to the *Charlotte* with a harrowing eyewitness account. By listening to the tales of people who lived in the harsh Arctic landscape, Hearne seized on a great chance to satisfy the curiosity that lingered over the expedition's destruction fifty years before. For that reason it is puzzling that no mention of the dramatic revelations are contained in the logs kept by either Stevens or Johnston. The only reference to the east harbour in either log is Johnston's 14 August entry noting: 'I sent the mate and 4 Hands to the East Harbour fore a few Coles our stock of firewood being allmost out.' The next day he added 'our boat returned with some Coals'. It was not until the publication of Hearne's 1795 narrative, *A Journey From Prince of Wales's Fort in Hudson's Bay To The Northern Ocean*, that the account of the deaths of Knight's men was recorded. The dawning sense of horror that greeted its first telling is palpable to this day.

The natives confirmed that Knight's storm-damaged ships had been driven into the harbour in late autumn 1719, and that the crews immediately began to build a shelter. At that time, the natives estimated their numbers at fifty, but when they returned the following summer the number of English was greatly reduced and the survivors seemed unhealthy. Despite their condition, the men were seen hard at work fashioning a longboat. Their desperate last bid for survival apparently failed. 'Sickness and famine occasioned such havoc among the English, that by the setting in of the second Winter their number was reduced to twenty,' Hearne was told. From their stone shelters erected on the opposite side of the harbour, the Inuit provided a temporary supply of whale's blubber and seal's flesh to Knight's men, before departing again in the spring of 1721. When the natives returned later that summer they found only five of the Englishmen alive.

In a state of starvation, the five survivors eagerly devoured the raw seal meat and whale blubber offered but 'this disordered them so much, that three of them died in a few days, and the other two, though very weak, made a shift to bury them', Hearne recorded. Then came the most disturbing story of all, one that seems to etch for ever the bounds of fellowship and suffering:

[They] survived many days after the rest, and frequently went to the top of an adjacent rock, and earnestly looked to the South and East, as if in expectation of some vessels coming to their relief. After continuing there a considerable time together, and nothing appearing in sight, they sat down close together, and wept bitterly. At length one of the two died, and the other's strength was so far exhausted, that he fell down and died also, in attempting to dig a grave for his companion.

Hearne himself viewed the skeletal remains of those last men, which he described as 'now lying above-ground close to the house'. By the account of the Inuit, the final breath passed from one who had fashioned iron into implements for them; 'probably he was the armourer, or smith', Hearne ended.

On Marble Island, this was the final image: bodies expended, nothing remaining but the emptiness and the cold.

8

A TIMELESS PLACE

Nothing has changed. Marble Island is the same landscape of death, the very same place where the brazen sails of chance sought refuge against the onslaught of winter almost three centuries ago. The long hours have for those many years passed unnoticed, as if time were in suspension, the stillness rarely interrupted. Occasionally a peregrine falcon darts from its cliff sanctuary or a sandhill crane ambles across a tundra bog. But for these few intrusions, and summer's brief interlude in the permanence of winter, time would cease to ebb entirely.

It was hoped that this slow rate of change would make it possible to step across the centuries to learn the truth of what happened to Captain James Knight at the place of his destruction. Lost documents, conflicting interpretations of historical records and a raft of questions believed unanswerable, have relegated Knight, his expedition and the circumstances surrounding the disaster to near obscurity. There is a body of scholarly work on Knight, but it is dwarfed by that devoted to virtually every other explorer to have ventured, however briefly, into Arctic waters. Popular historians have rarely mentioned Knight, and then it is usually only a cursory reference to justify the inclusion of Samuel Hearne's dramatic account of the death agony of the expedition's last survivors. More than being relegated to the marginalia of our history, for most of three centuries the Knight expedition has been forgotten.

Perhaps the failure of history is not surprising given the ambiguity of the circumstances of the expedition's disappearance, and the persistence of that mystery. The two theories of the

95

cause of the Knight disaster, while both seemingly plausible, are wholly at odds. The accepted version has come to be that provided by Hearne, whose chronicle of the death of forty men by 'sickness and famine' climaxes with the plight of the last survivors, searching the horizon for sails of salvation that never came. What makes Hearne's account especially disturbing is one historian's realization that those last men might actually have spotted the billowing sails of the *Prosperous*, with Kelsey aboard, in the summer of 1721, then watched in horror as it veered away. Those who have considered the mystery have generally favoured Hearne on the basis of little more than a sense that the mournful depiction seemed too real to have been a fiction; or by interpreting the representation of the last survivor suddenly collapsing as being how a victim of scurvy would expire, recalling the fate of Franklin's men, who 'fell down and died' as they walked. For Hearne, the tragedy was proof of the many dangers of discovery's desolate landscape, the expedition having been lost by virtue of the rigours of that 'inhospitable island, where neither stick nor stump was to be seen'.

Significantly, Hearne's explanation appears consistent with earlier reports. The Inuit boys who had been interviewed by Company factor Moses Norton in 1765 repeated strikingly similar tales of two ships wrecked many years before at Marble Island, and said that the crews, 'for want of Proper food, Clothing they Dwindled away very fast'. Indirect corroboration can also be drawn from Captain Francis Smith's report that during trading voyages to Whale Cove he was shown an 'English Man', a lad who appeared to be of 'a mixed Breed', which suggested to Smith that several of Knight's men might have actually survived for some time among the Inuit. All of these accounts portray the local Inuit as a benign presence, assisting the marooned crews as best they were able given the scarcity of food supplies, and perhaps even, at the Knight expedition's tragic finale, rescuing one or more of them from the edge of the abyss. It is a far cry from the massacre suggested by Master John Scroggs.

Some weight must be given to the fact that the disaster was still fresh when, in 1722, Scroggs visited Marble Island, the first

European to do so after Knight. Yet the later loss of Scroggs's logbook makes it impossible to tell what made him conclude that 'Every Man was Killed by the Eskemoes'. Given Indian rumours of Inuit violence, and long-held English suspicions about the 'thievish' tendencies of the unknown northerners, it is possible that Scroggs based his judgement entirely on the fact that the Inuit he encountered possessed relics from the missing expedition. That Scroggs failed to pursue not only the 'open sea' stretching west at Chesterfield Inlet, but also the fate of Knight, only confirmed to later critics his status as 'a timorous person' and further weakened the credibility of his conclusions. In Frederick Whymper's imaginative 1875 account *Heroes of the Arctic*, Scroggs's failure to 'search for these unfortunates' leads to the verdict that he 'deserves no place among our heroes'. To Hearne, Scroggs's circumstantial evidence did not even support the master's claim that he had been 'where the Albany and Discovery Sloop were both Ship-wracked'. Hearne argues in his *Journey* that the sum total of the items Scroggs had observed among the Inuit, a medicine chest, part of a mast, cabin lining and material from sails, 'scarcely amounted to the spoils which might have been made from a trifling accident, and consequently could not be considered as signs of a total shipwreck'.

But Hearne's own logic is at times inscrutable. He notes that the expedition was carrying a good stock of provisions, a house in frame and a great assortment of trading goods, while making no attempt to reconcile this apparent level of preparedness with the testimony of his elderly Inuit informants that at the conclusion of the first winter the crew numbers were already greatly diminished and the survivors seemed unhealthy. Hearne presents the testimony that only the larger of Knight's ships, the *Albany*, was seriously damaged 'in getting them into the harbour', only then to confirm that the hulls of both ships 'lie sunk in about five fathoms of water, toward the head of the harbour'. The castaways are next described by the Inuit to have been busily employed fashioning a longboat from ships' timbers for a last-ditch attempt to survive. Hearne himself saw evidence of the craft's construction as 'there is now lying a great quantity of oak chips, which have been most assuredly made by carpenters'.

While there is a curious authority to Hearne's reconstruction, each fragment of information only begs more questions. It is inconceivable that the crews would bide their time, as he would have it, over two miserable winters at their bleak refuge, gradually dying off from the effects of scurvy and starvation. Why would they not have made their escape from Marble Island to the mainland, just 15 kilometres away, then sallied down the coast to the new fort at the Churchill River, four days' sailing to the south? Or was Knight too proud to admit to 'Utmost Extreamity' and place himself at the mercy of Kelsey? To all of these questions, history has no answers.

Certainly Hearne provides no answer to the location of the scores of graves. Historians, extrapolating from Hearne's account of the heroic interment struggle of the last survivor, have commonly concluded that the bodies were scrupulously buried. In fact, besides the skull unearthed within the ruin, and Hearne's statement that the 'skulls and other large bones' of the last two to die 'are now lying above-ground close to the house', what few clues do survive to the location of the earthly remains of forty men are contained only in the vague, second-hand references in the journals of the whaling sloops that first visited the site in 1767. In the log of the *Success* Hearne is reported to have travelled to the 'New harbour for Coals and on their diging up part of a soft raising ground they found ye sculls & bones of Differant humane Bodies'. A reference in the *Churchill* log describes Hearne's discovery of 'A great Number of graves'. If the graves were anything like those typical of later European burials in the Arctic, they should have been clearly visible. The tombs of three members of the Franklin expedition dating from 1846 are unmistakable on the gravel shore of Beechey Island, with headboards and mounds covered with limestone slabs so that 'it breathes of the quiet churchyard in some of England's many nooks'. Similar attention was paid to the construction of the graves of members of Edward Belcher's 1852–4 expedition on Devon Island.

Since Knight's forty men died gradually over a period of

two years, there should be at least some surviving surface indication of a graveyard. Curiously, nothing has been seen of the graves since the report of their discovery; perhaps the only reason is that until Owen Beattie's own search, commencing two hundred and twenty years later, few had ever bothered to make the journey.

Integral to Beattie's research design for the Knight investigation were the methods and attitudes of modern forensic science. With money from the Boreal Institute for Northern Studies, he first assembled a modest research team in July 1989. The research was to be undertaken in phases, and the resources then grew gradually, reflecting the investigation results, and included support from the University of Alberta and the Social Sciences and Humanities Research Council of Canada. Just as he had done with his research into the Franklin expedition mystery, Beattie intended to apply to the Knight investigation the forensic anthropological techniques he had previously employed in examining the carnage and complex identification problems resulting from train and air crashes. The focus of these cases has been to ascertain the identity of victims, and provide information that could assist in determining cause and manner of death, and ultimately responsibility and accountability. But where the Knight mass disaster stands apart from the Franklin research is in its resemblance to another area of focus for practitioners of the forensic sciences, the crime scene.

Because of the conflicting historical testimony regarding the cause of the Knight expedition's destruction, and because of the potential for evidence of violence, it provided a rare opportunity to apply to a centuries-old Arctic mystery methodology identical to that Beattie had previously used to assist medical examiners, Crown prosecutors and law enforcement agencies, including the Royal Canadian Mounted Police, in numerous criminal investigations. In the practice of such investigations, Beattie has rarely found himself analysing well-preserved bones or identifiable bodies. More often the cases involve bodies burned and decomposed beyond recognition or dismembered and stripped by animals. In one notorious instance a homicide victim's body had been intentionally burned for three days, the charred bones then being crushed by the wheels of a front-end loader which was used to scatter the remains over acres of farmland in an attempt to eliminate criminal evidence. Often in the investigation of such scenes, human remains constitute only one of several independent lines of evidence.

Through application of the new hybrid science, forensic archaeology, Beattie further hoped to identify additional information, even the most minute clue. As a result, over the four field seasons the ranks of the researchers broadened from the preliminary team, which included expedition assistant Bill Gawor, archaeological field assistant Martin Amy, and student field assistants David Tatuiini and Feliks Kappi, to involve sixteen researchers and assistants representing a variety of fields of study: anthropology, archaeology, clothing science, geology and history. A resident of Rankin Inlet whose varied experience includes incarnations as an art student, miner, head of the local crisis line and hamlet councillor, Gawor possessed specialized knowledge of the land and a painter's eye which provided a necessary counterpoint to scientific observation.

The first question Beattie faced was whether after such a great interlude, there would be surviving human remains. Because of the obvious implications of a graveyard on any interpretation, the initial phase involved the search for and documentation of archaeological sites fitting the historical testimony of one witness, the second-hand account of Samuel Hearne's discovery of 'A great Number of graves'. Historical evidence was crucial to identifying sites and understanding the disaster, but what did not matter were the age-old interpretations arising from that evidence. It was only when identified sites were dismantled systematically, the appearance, sequence and associations of individual evidence considered and inconsistencies identified, that any investigator could begin to assume the status of expert witness. In that sense, Beattie set out to become his own witness.

The archaeological surveys were initiated in 1989, continued in 1990 and completed in 1991. Once scenes relevant to the Knight expedition were identified, they were dismantled; as a result, excavations overlapped the period of survey,

Aerial view of the massive stone ruins of Prince of Wales's Fort which was founded by Captain James Knight.

Inuit tradition dictates that first-time visitors to any of the islands in the Marble Island group should crawl up the beach on their elbows and knees. Left to right: Feliks Kappi , Martin Amy, John Geiger and Bill Gawor.

John Geiger standing by one of the more elaborate graves in the nineteenth-century American whalers' cemetery on Dead Man's Island.

The dramatic rubble fields of Marble Island.

The dark green area in the centre is the foundation of Knight's house on Quartzite Island.

Walt Kowal taking notes during excavations of Knight's house in 1991. The wooden corner post, which was sawn off by Inuit, and the wall, showing the interlaced pattern of sod, can both be seen clearly.

A pair of brass dividers found on the floor of Knight's house during the excavation.

Feliks Kappi displaying the silver Danish coin that he discovered. It dates from 1644.

A coin found during excavations in Knight's house.

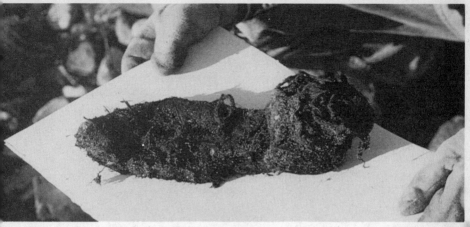

ne of the leather boots found in Knight's house.

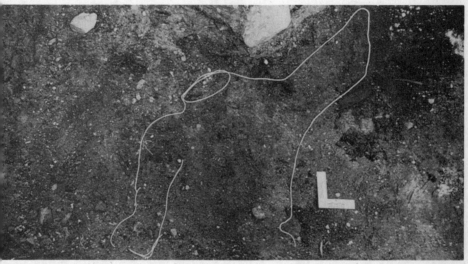

he string depicts the partly visible outline of a large piece of fabric, thought to be a
hirt.

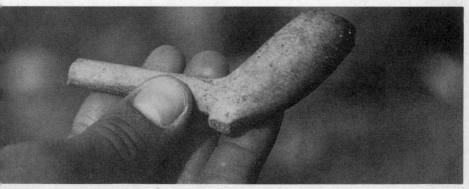

well preserved clay pipe bowl and part of the stem.

Divers Don Palfrey and Jeff Gilmour preparing to explore the remains of Knight's ships.

Conducting sonar scans in the harbour where Knight's ships are located.

Part of the hull of the *Albany* frigate showing the splash guard.

An *inukshuk* on a small island between Marble Island and the mainland. These stacks of rock made in the shape of human beings are found throughout the eastern Arctic.

Silhouette of Bill Gawor and radio antennae, reminiscent of the many *inukshuk* seen in this region.

beginning in 1989, concentrated in 1990 and completed in 1991. The analysis of the recovered artefacts and information ran concurrently with the archaeology, beginning in late 1989 and continuing to 1993. Each expedition had its remarkable occurrences, but more remarkable still was the perspective provided by the fullness of the research. The team lived for those seasons on a silent landscape that seemed a metaphor for the mysteries played out there, viewing the hard, tempestuous climate, the strangeness of the plants and wildlife, in much the way Knight's men must have done centuries earlier, as wondrous yet somehow malignant. Still, as the consequence of the breadth of the investigation, they were able to visit the mystery at its very source.

They embarked at the head of Rankin Inlet, in the community of the same name, for the crossing of the nearly 50 kilometres of grey water to the eastern coast of Marble Island. Rankin Inlet was established in 1955 as a mining centre by North Rankin Nickel Mines, which closed only seven years later, leaving behind a massive concentrator that still dominates the hamlet skyline, indifferent to the economic blow suffered by the mine's closure. Still the community of about eighteen hundred has overcome the set-back, today serving as a regional transportation and administrative centre in the eastern Arctic. Ironically, in July 1989 the retail hub of the community remained the same corporation for which James Knight had devoted a lifetime of service: the Hudson's Bay Company.

In all, the journey from Rankin Inlet into Hudson Bay was made four times, from 1989 to 1992, and it was never uneventful. During the second field season, in 1990, the voyage proved particularly harrowing. Driven by two high-powered outboard engines, the yawl tacked gently along the mainland coast sheltered from the large waves, before the pilot suddenly pointed full throttle into heavy seas. The fibreglass boat shuddered under the impact of each wave. Soon team members were sitting on their hands to cushion each shock. When the waves were swelling to over two metres, and it was apparent that the pilot was not about to slow down, Bill Gawor and the project archaeologist, Walt Kowal, crawled into the nose to add weight. There they could actually see the hull flex under the concussions. After more than an hour what first appeared to be a wreath of ice finally materialized on the horizon. It was Marble Island, half the time obscured by waves. Only when the boat cruised along the island's south coast did the water calm, and the roar of the engines slow. The boat continued to the east, searching for the first sight of the point where the island would end and Hudson Bay would again stretch uninterrupted to the horizon. It was on the coast before that point in 1767 that the harpooners from the *Success* had nosed their boat through an opening in the rock and discovered the last refuge of the Knight expedition.

The curtain of stone was now drawn, each jetty passed immediately replaced with another. In the same water, in 1989, the grey curl of a wave was split by the arc of a white whale only metres from the bow. Soon, in the distance, was what may have been another. Luke Foxe had described the waters of Marble Island as alive with whales, but those were bowheads, and in the centuries that followed whalers too discovered the sanctuary. That species has for commercial purposes been extirpated from Hudson Bay. Today the beluga swims alone. Suddenly the engines were shut down and pulled up. With a spotter on the bow, the yawl crept by the shoals towards shore near the opening to the cove, finally touching the island's stone face. Before long the boat had turned away and the roar of the outboard engines was replaced by the rhythmic drumming of the wind on hooded jackets. Each team member then respected the dictates of legend and preserved the sanctity of the dead by crawling up the stone beach on elbows and knees.

The island is at times deceptive in its beauty. Its sudden appearance, and stone 'all of a white Marble', transfixed Foxe, its European discoverer, in 1631. It has the same effect today. Hearne described Marble Island as 'that inhospitable island', and while it is a desolate outcrop, hundreds of kilometres north of the tree line, it in no way resembles the place, destitute of life, sometimes employed to explain the Knight tragedy. Foxe reported that the ships' dog gave chase to a 'reine deer' and recorded the discovery of a 'young Tall Fowle' on the island, mistaking it for an ostrich. His master suggested it was a stork, but it was almost certainly a sandhill crane. Cranes nest on Marble Island to this day. One early evening in August 1991 a pair swooped gracefully over Knight's ruin, the air filled with their strange cries. Theodore Swaine Drage, clerk of the *California*, in 1746 gaped at the abundant life – geese, swans, ducks, and a variety of other wild fowl – noting that 'there were not less than two hundred swimming at the Entrance of the Cove'.

Historical accounts abound with such descriptions of the island's wildlife and the intervening years have changed little. There is an astonishing diversity of life. Around the saltwater margins, white-rumped sandpipers and golden plovers preen, while the freshwater ponds are alive with red-throated and Arctic loons, oldsquaw and king eider ducks and large numbers of Canada geese. Drage had reported 'a great Number of Seals, and of a larger Size than any we had seen before, remarkably grey with large Whiskers'. It is presumably a reference to bearded seals, *ugjuk*, which continue to inhabit island waters, along with ringed seals, walrus and belugas. Land mammals still sighted include Arctic foxes and hares, and at dusk on 12 August 1991, the distant gait of a polar bear seen at a kilometre's distance by two crew members. A watch was struck and two hours later warning shots were fired, startling those who had retired. The entire team assembled just as the great animal once again ambled out of view, this time never to return. Instead, before them unfolded the aurora borealis, Knight's 'petty dancers', arched in pale green directly over the expedition's ruined shelter, seeming to touch the quartzite outcrop beyond. It was as if they had been summoned to see their dance.

The first days of the 1989 archaeological survey ended in perplexity. Nothing remotely resembled an expedition grave-yard. Beattie pored over Hearne's published account of the expedition, and the frustrating accounts given by Johnston and Stevens, and in the case of the latter, struggled to make sense of the clue of the 'soft raising ground' in its actual geographical context. It seemed to apply to elevation, like a gentle slope, but could also reflect the firmness of the surface itself. In either regard it failed to yield a solution. Time and again the ritual was repeated: each slight depression, each unusual feature, excavated to sterile ground. Even the microscopic study of high-resolution black and white photographs taken at a low altitude of 3000 feet, and providing visibility of objects as small as 20–30 centimetres, failed to locate any pattern that would suggest burials.

The search for the site of the graveyard began in the area of the expedition shelter, and spread out in an ever-greater radius. The foot survey was carried out by parties numbering as few as three to as many as seven members, and was conducted primarily over two summer field seasons lasting from late July to the third week of August, in 1989 and 1990. Together team members saw a landscape virtually unchanged since Hearne's time, gaining not only an understanding of the geography and biology, but also a window on at least five centuries of human history and prehistory. Yet the mystery remained. The shadow of the expedition was only readily manifest with Knight's shelter. Even in its ruinous state, the landmark attests to something of significance having transpired there, something reduced to a distant memory yet to be awakened.

Minor expedition sites were located within 500 metres of the shelter ruin. Remarkably, on the harbour's south face, pockets of wood chips remain where long ago 'carpenters were at work'. Directly opposite, on a slope near the ruin, a large pattern of white stones laid on the pale green moss, and roughly in the shape of an eight, is clearly visible. Traces confirmed its relationship to the expedition. There was brick, coal and, nearly missed, a bracket-shaped iron artefact that poked through the mat of vegetation. By its location, on the north side of the cove and within sight of the shelter, the feature might have represented the site of a storage tent. Further north the landscape was unrelenting, a succession of broken, grey-gravel beaches abutting low, white outcrops. The monotony was only occasionally interrupted by a bright pocket of northern fireweed, the shock of an oldsquaw fleeing its nest or the discovery of the fiercely armed skull of an Arctic fox. Each

Eighteenth-century view of the creatures of Hudson Bay.

variation in the repetition seemed to take on great significance, but only one had any.

At the point where the ridge sloped towards the north entrance to the cove there was a ring of stones, laid out like a pearl necklace, and tiny white objects – a broken clay pipe. The stones represented the outline where a tent once stood. A lone red brick was identical to those at Knight's shelter. 'It's a lookout,' Gawor said, gesturing towards the Bay. From there the Bay's pewter waters reached across the horizon, the inland sea's vastness taxing even the imagination. A dirty band to the north-west indicated the mainland, then to the north and east, only water and sky. 'But they were supposed to be looking south, not north,' Beattie said. Yet its appearance did remind him of the point from which the last survivors were supposed to have seen the sails that, it is argued, could have saved them.

As abruptly as this evidence for human habitation begins, it ends. The vast stone landscape spread out, its harshness muted as huge, jagged boulders gave way to smooth stone faces cradling crystal-clear ponds, some lined with beaches of fine quartzite sand. To understand the geography it is important to know that the name Marble Island was historically applied not to one island, but to a group of four islands. Technically the Knight disaster did not occur on Marble Island at all, but a much smaller isle immediately to the east that has been assigned the descriptive, if uninspired name Quartzite Island. Shaped like a spear point, Quartzite Island stretches four kilometres to its easternmost tip. At low tide the shallow sea rushes over the stones at the entrances to the cove that separates it from the larger island, mimicking the chatter of whitewater in a mountain stream. Only then do the two islands again become one, connected by land bridges at either end of the cove.

It is a rough crossing to Marble Island. At places the race of the tide is furious, making each step slow and purposeful. The gentle beach of the large island sweeps up to a stone plateau that stretches the island's breadth. The great outcrops were interrupted by eskers, dunes of stone sliding down into sheer divides. Beyond the superficial constancy of rock was surprising diversity. Even the colour changed. Mostly the quartzite was

the sterile white of a hospital room, but at other times, faint pink
or splashed with tawny stains. Just once, there was the brilliant
green of malachite. There was an eeriness to the landscape. In
the half-light of dusk, which reached late into the evening, or
once, on 20 July 1989, when a full moon lifted above the rim of
the earth and cast its pale light, the stone took on the ghostly
burnish of white marble.

The effect of weather also altered the way the land was seen.
Luke Foxe's haunting memory of beauty is preserved by Marble
Island's biology, its varied species of birds and bright stands of
Arctic poppies, when the sun shoots up and a breeze keeps
the mosquitoes crouched low to the tundra. But the weather is
highly variable, and the change comes violently. One storm of
tremendous severity struck the camp on 23 July 1989. Winds
shift, and suddenly it is very cold. Then you cannot see the
flowers, or hear the birds. What you see are the rocks and the
stone, the richness of their texture lost with the light. At the
end of vision, Hudson Bay, which earlier had the stillness of
a lake, became a sea again, the roar of breakers vying with the
howl of the wind. At midnight the rhythm of the storm shook
the tents with fierce pulls and blasts. At four a.m., charged
with electricity, its full fury hit. Lashes of thunder ripped
through the camp. Everyone lay exposed to the nightmare,
frozen inside their tents, counting . . . one one thousand, two
one thousand . . . Lightning fell within a 650-metre radius. Each
surge of rain was followed again. One one thousand, two . . .
Closer, a 450-metre radius. The stone has many faces. But for
that one night, bathed by an electrical storm, it looked pallid,
and suddenly finite.

Evidence of five centuries of human occupation and endeavour was revealed by the survey of the islands, allowing not only
an understanding of the different phases of life visited upon
the landscape, but also unique insight into the process of time.
The Knight expedition should not be viewed in isolation from
other human activity; rather it was part of a continuum, being
both influenced by, and an influence on, others. The pattern
of occupation falls into three sequential phases, excluding
Knight's own: the activities of nineteenth-century American

and British whalers, the height of Inuit occupation in the eighteenth century and the ancient Thule sites, centuries older. By studying each Beattie gained information immediately relevant to the Knight investigation and developed an understanding of the processes of decay and disintegration which allowed interpretation of how the expedition site changed over time.

The first evidence of the most recent of these occupations was found when the ranges of desolation fell away into a vale of green at the midpoint of Quartzite Island. Everywhere were relics of the forgotten. Student assistant David Tatuiini located a large stone circle, asking Beattie, 'Is it from Knight?' Beattie's first thought was that this must have been related to the expedition, as the tent feature was not Inuit. Ten metres to the south lay a makeshift tomb. Large slabs were assembled to mark the grave. It was the kind of burial Beattie had expected to mark the graveyard of Knight's crews. A human femur was found lying on the surface, and lichen growing on the exposed side indicated that the disturbance had come long ago. Other bone fragments were scattered nearby, as was the blade of a knife. The discovery was unsettling. Soon stems and bowls of broken clay pipes, which lay exposed on the surface, provided the first clues to the site's origin. The bones were not of one of the missing explorers, but of an American whaler. A chronicle of their visit survives in the square-headed nails, badly rusted barrel hoops, and bricks, different from those found at Knight's harbour. Also scattered over the site were fragments of old tin cans typical of the mid-nineteenth century. Perhaps this man was sent to an icy death by the thrashing of a wounded whale, perhaps he had died twisted in agony from scurvy. Still, he was not alone.

For several decades during the nineteenth century, the island's west-end harbour, separated from Knight's harbour by 10 kilometres, became a winter home for American, and some British, harpooners, their frigid isolation spent battling scurvy and boredom. There were diversions. In 1867 men from New Bedford's *Orray Taft* unwittingly came across the site of the Knight disaster. Their main interest was not with the mysterious relics but in the 'bed of coal that had been left

Whaling in Hudson Bay in the nineteenth century (top).
Whalers' winter quarters at west harbour, Marble Island (bottom).

109

there some time ago'. The Americans promptly laid claim to this 'discovery', the assertion of ownership being solely for the benefit of the crew of the competing British whaler *Ocean Nymph*, which had been sent to revive the Hudson's Bay Company's whaling interests and was suspected to be short of fuel. What followed ranks as one of the silliest episodes of Anglo-American relations. Hearing of the coal find, British crewmen ignored the American claim and gathered some of the fuel for themselves. The act so infuriated the American captain, who had been stewing over the haughty behaviour of the British ever since their arrival, remarking that if their imperiousness 'is English fashion, keep me from England', that he had his men collect up as much coal as they could use, then burn about 'two tons' of what remained.

When the whalers were not squabbling over coal, they were acting out their aggression. An 1865 sketch depicts a performance of the 'Marble Island Minstrels' starring men dressed up as an 'Artic [*sic*] elephant' or walrus, with 'Carl Carendo' and 'John Bull' – caricatures of an Italian and Englishman – in supporting roles. A more ambitious production, Sheridan's *Pizarro*, was also staged. The veteran Massachusetts whaling captain and sometime theatre critic George Parker decided, only partly in jest, that 'tragedy is their forte'. A survey of the area in 1884 confirmed this ghastly truth, leaving the gentleman-explorer Charles Tuttle 'surprised at seeing so many indications of the dead'. He was not referring to any east-end graves of Knight's men, but the tombs of the American whalers laid out in rows on the islet near their winter harbour, 'their poor bodies upon these cold rocks where the winds of almost perpetual winter blow in pitiless and withering blasts'.

There is a precedent for a European-style graveyard at Marble Island. During six hellish months in 1873, fourteen American whalemen from the barks *Ansel Gibbs* and *Orray Taft* died at their winter harbour from the ravaging effects of scurvy. Even in October 1872, before the dreaded cold of winter set in, they were undermined by an inadequate food supply and a growing sick list. It was only a matter of time before scurvy broke out. Veteran officers watched incredulously as the young

A whaler's sketch of an 1865 theatrical performance of
'The Artic Elephant', performed by the Marble Island Minstrels.

crewmen refused to eat the flesh of foxes, concluding that they would 'rather lay and die'. In February, a twenty-four-year-old became the first. Even at − 40°C and with the crew crippled by disease, a grave was dug. By May, with the temperature still near freezing-point, a string of graves were neatly arranged on the gravel islet near the harbour entrance, now called by the name once applied to all of Marble Island – Dead Man's Island. Those burials are today little changed from when they were constructed during a grim winter more than a century ago. The shipmates of the dead laid large stones over the grave mounds. In several cases, smaller, pure white stones, were then neatly assembled to delineate the burial. The foot of each grave is followed by the head of the next, creating a ridge stretching the breadth of the small island. Originally the fourteen graves were each numbered with a marker of wood, and at the midpoint a large cairn was erected with a plaque denoting the names of the dead by number.

Near the graves, on the bald face of stone within the narrow gut that forms the entrance to the whalers' harbour, is an unrelated memorial, discovered in 1879 during a stop-off by members of Frederick Schwatka's search for clues to the destruction of Sir John Franklin's expedition. Seven names are written in red paint and a date: 1787. A member of Schwatka's party wondered whether it could be 'a gigantic tombstone to record those who perished here long ago by shipwreck'. Subsequent research proved it was nothing more than two-century-old graffiti, painted to mark one of the succession of visits paid to Marble Island by the Hudson's Bay Company's sloop *Churchill*. But together with the carefully constructed graves of the whalemen, it attests to something else: the ease with which this stark landscape can preserve the memory of human presence.

The most pervasive evidence of occupation belongs to the people of the region, the Inuit. Numerous individual sites were identified during the survey, but one stood out from all the others, both by its vast scale and its direct bearing on the Knight investigation. Across the eastern harbour from where Knight wintered, Hearne described sighting the remains of an encampment where 'some of the Esquimaux took up their abode', the place from which the survivors presumably bartered for the whale blubber and seal meat that ultimately only prolonged their hope, and their suffering. Hearne concluded that the Inuit camp would 'in all probability . . . be discernible for many years to come'. No traces survive on the land directly opposite Knight's ruin, but where a low, marshy area forced the survey team into the lee of vast outcrops, where the wind dropped to stillness and the sun was eclipsed, they came upon a scattering of Inuit crypts.

Large slabs were carefully laid up to nearly a metre from the ground, covering each grave, which unlike so many in the north, remained undisturbed through succeeding ages. Only one had partially collapsed, but the damage had been wrought by time, not scavenging animals. Peering through a small opening in the stones, Beattie could see the skull and bones of one who had died centuries before. As each man stood in silence for an interval, it was impossible not to be moved by the thought that this garden of stone was a sacred ground. The divergence of culture is never so evident as in the

Dead Man's Island, with its grim ridge of graves
belonging to nineteenth-century New England whalers.

113

treatment of the dead; and perhaps no burial appeared so final as this.

It is little wonder Hearne believed the remains of the Inuit structures would be discernible for years to come. More than two centuries later, they still endure. It is a remarkable site. In a society where typical groups or encampments numbered some ten to twenty-five people, there are well over a hundred, perhaps as many as two hundred, structures to the south of the crypts, stretching into the distance. 'It's like a city,' Beattie said, 'and as old as one.' The site had been occupied for a considerable time, not only Knight's own, but one measured in centuries. The major occupation was located along a high beach ridge separated from the shore of the harbour by a steep embankment. Along this ridge are the stone remains of many houses, some larger communal structures, kayak rests, food caches and more graves. Upslope and inland there are successive parallel beach ridges, waves of gravel, each possessing groupings of structures, the oldest beach ridges now high above the present water-line, and farther from the most recent occupation. What science has determined with reasonable certainty is that large camps such as that on Marble Island were made up of houses used in the spring and autumn, during the transitional months between summer inland caribou hunts and occupation of winter snowhouse villages. As recently as the 1930s, several sleds of the Qairnirmiut, the local people, still arrived each spring to harpoon whales at the floe's edge.

What little is known of the lives of those who inhabited the north-west coast of Hudson Bay in the eighteenth century comes from a handful of accounts from the first period of European contact. Frightened silly by the very appearance of the northerners, most contemptuously dismissed them as a brutish people living a crude, 'vagabond life'. Such facile judgments, tainted by ignorance and racism, had taken root in the Western consciousness. There is to be found, however, one notable exception: a portrayal of the Inuit more in keeping with the assumption of enlightenment we generously ascribe to ourselves. In his 1748 narrative *A Voyage to Hudson's Bay by the Dobbs Galley and California*, Henry Ellis marvels at a people who survived with the benefit of few raw materials. But in their spear points and float harpoons, their kayaks and snow-goggles, their 'neat, and even elegant' seal and caribou-skin clothing, Ellis detected a rare 'spirit of invention'. Someday, he predicted, we would come to know them better, and perhaps then 'consider them in another Light'.

Inuit bone scattered at the site came from a series of disturbed burials. During a visit to the Inuit camp in August 1990, Walt Kowal was convinced that the bone had been mistaken for the 'great Number of graves' first reported by Hearne in 1767, and recorded in the sloop logs. A veteran of Beattie's previous investigation into the Franklin disaster, Kowal had spearheaded the lead-isotope studies which traced the source of lead in the bodies of Franklin crewmen to that expedition's tinned food. Now he had supported Beattie's suspicion of a possible link between the reference to Knight expedition graves and Inuit

Inuit family on the north-west coast of Hudson Bay, date 1746/7.

burials. No one knew it at the time, but the speculation was later backed by a curious historical reference, notably that of Captain Charles Duncan, of the Royal Navy, who was the next European after Hearne to visit Marble Island, twenty-two years later.

In response to renewed rumours that the Hudson's Bay Company was withholding from the public the probability of a Northwest Passage, Duncan was equipped by the Company and sent from London by the Admiralty to search the north-west coast of Hudson Bay, particularly Corbett and Chesterfield inlets, for the passage to the western ocean. On 28 August 1791, with the brig *Beaver* anchored at Marble Island, Duncan and his mate, George Taylor, travelled to the east end of the island 'to View the harbour we had heard of'. Taylor describes collecting 'a piece of carved work of a ships stern that has been wrecked here'.

Unfortunately, whatever information might have been gleaned from Duncan's journal was lost. The captain had been con-vinced he would be hailed as the discoverer of the elusive Northwest Passage and was so despondent at his failure that he was fit to be tied, and was, to his bunk. The precaution proved fruitless, as he felt the disappointment of his defeat so severely 'that whilst on his voyage home he was attack'd with a Brain Fever, the effect of which wholly prevented him from delivering a Journal of his Voyage'.

What has survived is a hitherto unpublished letter written before Duncan's affliction, while the *Beaver* wintered at the Churchill River in September 1791. He recounted for the Governor and Committee of the Company observations of the disaster scene, observations probably of only passing interest at the time, but which now take on a particular significance:

That there has been a vessel, or vessels, cast away at the Island is very evident, for I saw a part of two anchors, a quantity of Bricks & Human Bones, lie among Fish Bones, where the Esquimeaux have resided. It is not likely, that they would let the Bones of their own Countrymen lie exposed.

The bricks found are in the immediate vicinity of the Knight ruin, but the reference to bone is stated as being where the 'Esquimeaux have resided'. This can only be interpreted as a reference to the Inuit village across the harbour, where human bone from disturbed, centuries-old surface graves is visible 'among Fish Bones' to this day. The implication of Duncan's letter is that the pervasive signs of Inuit activity in the use of wood and iron from the expedition, and the presence of Inuit bone at the site so near to that occupied by Knight's crews, confused still further those attempting to understand the nature of the mystery. The discovery of Duncan's letter gave credence to the possibility that Hearne could have made such a fundamental error, mistaking Inuit burials in the area for Knight's 'graves'. It is at least notable that when the time came for Hearne to record his own observations of the grim discoveries made at Marble Island, no graveyard is mentioned.

Appearing like a fallen white temple, a scene of colossal destruction, is the bluff that makes up the easternmost limit of Quartzite Island. Stone can trick the eye into seeing clusters of columns and marble friezes, as if monuments to a lost culture. Early explorers habitually drew such comparisons between the familiar landscapes of Europe and the unrelentingly foreign lands they encountered in the north. It was a way to provide orientation, to make the unknown recognizable. But such analogies are always misleading. This is not a sun-drenched Aegean island, and the only true ruins on the escarpment belong to the last, and to the earliest, period of human occupation: that of the Thule, prehistoric inhabitants of the realms of ice. Ancestors of the Inuit, the Thule migrated across the Arctic regions of North America from Alaska around AD 1000. Effective techniques for hunting large whales and a milder climate allowed them to establish a relatively sedentary existence that gave rise to a unique and complex culture. Few Europeans encountered the Thule before that culture vanished with the advent of the period of climatic cooling. By Knight's time, only ruins remained to tell of their existence.

Dyonyse Settle's 1578 account of Martin Frobisher's third

voyage provides only a startled glimpse of the 'people of the countrie', describing their 'leaping and dancing with straunge shrikes and cryes'. In one violent episode, Frobisher himself was struck with an iron-tipped Thule arrow. What little else is known comes from the study of artefacts and the remains of small villages like that discovered at the island's eastern headland.

It was a winter village, the imposing stone foundations of each oval house measuring 4–5 metres across. Still visible are interior divisions, a living and cooking chamber, and raised flagstone sleeping platform. The entrance is built of rock slabs. A roof framed in whale ribs and jawbones and covered with skins and turf once provided perfect insulation. Much of the culture that had developed around the blubber lamps, the songs, dances and ceremonies – the wisdom – is now lost. Only rare ivory carvings or elaborately worked tools, and toy tops made from whale vertebrae, survive to attest to the culture's achievements. A cursory survey of the village failed to reveal any such artefacts. There were only the houses, caches, walrus skulls and the crypts of the Thule. In one partially disturbed burial were the bones of an adolescent girl, still at rest in the lonely place of her death.

All this evidence is available to the eye: whalers' graves, Inuit graves, even Thule graves. What the archaeological survey had not revealed were those which Beattie had sought, presumably the single largest grouping of all, the graves of Knight's men. Huge *inuksuit* stand on the smooth roof of the headland. These stacks of rock made in the shape of human beings are found throughout the eastern Arctic, their significance known only to those who built them. Perhaps they were signposts to show in winter that this white island was not of ice. But there was nothing to resemble an explorer's cairn. No signposts indicating the whereabouts of forty men. This is where Knight should have stationed his watch: land's edge, with streams of clouds spilling over the horizon, and at their back the cool face of the setting sun.

Had there been a readily identifiable graveyard, had the graves accounted for most expedition members and had studies of the bone revealed the surface scaling and pitting characteristic of Vitamin C deficiency, the cause of scurvy, then Hearne's hypothesis for the expedition's destruction would have been supported by physical evidence. Past reconstructions of the Knight disaster have used the reference to 'A great Number of graves' as proof of the accuracy of the natives' accounts of slow death by starvation and scurvy. But the certainty of the past is rarely glimpsed so easily. The futile search yielded nothing to lend credence to the historical interpretation that 'A great Number of graves' equated with a cemetery.

9

The LAST MAN

The point of departure for the investigation came with the decision to dig randomly selected test pits over the large area surrounding Knight's ruin and to undertake the excavation of the structure itself. The cove in which the expedition sought refuge is a forgotten corner of history preserved in exquisite detail. Here, as perhaps nowhere else in the landscape of discovery, was an opportunity to investigate relics directly associated with the age of northern exploration; evidence which, either because of its geographical isolation or the relative silence of historical inquiry, has survived to the present. It was among those early-eighteenth-century tools and ornaments, food debris and clothing fragments, that witness to the untold stories of the Knight expedition lay.

In their search for clues to the identity and fate of the men who once occupied the site, the whalers in 1767 turned to Knight's ruin for answers. Now Beattie's investigation had taken him to the same place. On 9 August 1990 a small force of field assistants began archaeological excavations, the nature of which one of them, near the end of eleven days of continuous work, likened to 'convict labour'. The torment was not limited to the difficult, time-consuming dig itself, or even the plagues of mosquitoes excited into a frenzy by the activity and sweat. Rather it lay in the danger that in a moment of carelessness or distraction some meaningful evidence would be overlooked, the context of an artefact ignored, as a consequence leaving the puzzle perhaps incomplete for ever. The significance of the site was lost on no one. Here could prove to be the last that anyone would ever know of the fate of Captain James Knight.

Stark evidence of previous disturbance was seen in the scars to sod and moss within the ruin's foundation. The major disturbance was the earliest, and involved the dismantling of the superstructure for its raw materials by the Inuit immediately after the expedition's period of occupation. The next diggings were exploratory, conducted by the whalers in 1767. A century later, American whalers, like the Inuit salvagers before, exploited the site for raw materials, digging into and hauling away coal, and destroying much of what fuel remained. The site again faded from memory for more than a century, until it was revisited in 1970 and again in 1971, when pioneering exploratory archaeological excavations were conducted. These investigations reaffirmed the site's origin, yielding lids from small kegs, staves and willow hoops, fragments of wine and medicine bottles, pipe stems and a brick feature. Except for the most recent workings, the disturbances themselves have been transformed by time into part of the archaeological record, in one such instance providing an invaluable clue to the time of year of the death, or disappearance, of the last Knight expedition survivors.

Walt Kowal identified the first significant piece of evidence, one which had been overlooked by the whalers. During his investigation of the site in 1767, Magnus Johnston noted in the log of the *Churchill* that the ruin once had a wooden frame, 'and its very plain to be seen, Now every hole where the posts stood, which is all Dugg out and gone By the Esquimaux'. What Johnston had neglected to mention was that while the posts were indeed removed by the Inuit, the base of the posts remained in the ground, the chop marks, from hand-held stone tools, still visible. Rather than dig out the large, 20-centimetre-diameter structural posts around the exterior walls, as well as the smaller, 15-centimetre interior supports, they were cut nearly four-fifths of the way through with evident difficulty just above the floor level, even though the posts went little more than 30–60 centimetres into the ground. The last, uncut portion was broken as the post was physically pulled down. From this it is clear that the structure was dismantled, and its wood recovered, when the ground was still frozen. It would not have been possible to pull the posts out without first digging into the rock-hard frozen ground. Paramount to any new understanding of the Knight mystery was the collection of such practical evidence. In this case, coupled with archaeological and historical information about the residency patterns of area Inuit, it is evidence of the dereliction of the structure in spring or autumn.

Of nearly equal importance in ascertaining the length of the expedition's stay at the site was a determination of the time of year of the shelter's construction. The use of several tons of local material for the foundation, the dominant surviving visible feature, was good evidence that the structure was erected before the onset of winter in late September. The foundation consists primarily of many hundreds of large rocks and boulders stripped from the surface of the immediate vicinity. Elongated oval ditches abutting three sides likewise provided fill as well as rocks and boulders for the foundation. These ditches, 0.75 metre deep, could not have been easily dug when the ground was frozen. None of the hundreds of red bricks that now lie scattered around its periphery was part of the foundation itself. The shape is rectangular, with the long axis running NW to SE. Strangely, it is oriented obliquely to the shore, and was probably positioned to minimize the effects of the prevailing north-westerly winds. Measuring from the foundation's high points, the structure is 14.4 metres long and 9 metres wide. The foundation has partially collapsed both inside and outside, with the width of the slumped walls, from the high point, ranging between 1 metre and 1.5 metres outward, and approximately 1 metre inward. The top of the foundation sits on average 1.25 metres higher than the surrounding surface.

One feature associated with the ruin stands out. The south-west corner has been built up with a significantly greater number of large rocks and boulders. A great deal of speculation was offered about its function. The rock pile was taken apart in the hope that something underneath would reveal its purpose, but there were no hints. Adjacent to this is the only breach in the exterior wall, measuring slightly more than 0.5 metre wide. A low, L-shaped mound of earth fronts this opening, and has the characteristics of an entrance airlock. The opening would have faced south-east, the least common wind direction. In 1767 Johnston noted the proximity of the large coal pile to this feature, which he described as the 'dore of the House', certain evidence 'that they have Endeaver'd to mak a defence against The Cold of the winter'.

The severe climate of the region required such precautions. The nearest weather records to Marble Island, kept by factor Richard Staunton at the new fort on the Churchill River, suggest the winter of 1719–20 was in keeping with a period of climatic cooling, predictably harsh. 'The wind at n. blowing hard, and drifting Snow & So verry Cold,' bemoans Staunton on 25 November, in a typical entry. As late as May he grimly recorded the death of a Company servant, 'his Eyes & Teeth Sett, being numbd & Blowted with the Cold'. Little remains of the expedition's vast coal pile, which is now delineated by a large, irregularly shaped black scar on the surface, although in 1767 the coal pile was estimated at not less than seven or eight chaldrons (9.1–10.4 cubic metres) of the original twenty (26 cubic metres) loaded aboard the *Albany*, a good indication that the site was occupied for one winter.

Since the discovery of the ruined shelter, no one has been able to accurately ascertain its original appearance. The excavations conducted in the structure in 1990, and continued in 1991, uncovered enough surviving architectural features to finally permit a reconstruction. Immediately below the 10–15-centimetre blanket of sod many fragments of wood and wood planking were found, representing the collapsed roof and exterior and interior wall sheathing. Underlying this material was a variably thick, highly organic layer, composed of the sod stripped from the ground around the structure and used to insulate the exterior walls, which through previous disturbance now contains some bricks and artefacts. Below this layer is a thin (1–3 centimetres) greasy black, highly organic film covering the actual floor of the structure and representing the daily accumulation of detritus and soot. The grimy nature of the film is telling of the environment in which those who inhabited the structure lived and the accuracy of Knight's complaint, made while serving as Governor, that: 'wee being stowd up in a Close House all the winter, what with the stoves, Lamps, Tobacco Smoaking and Dressing of Victualls . . . it is very Unwholesom.' Yet the filth provided perhaps the unlikeliest clue of all, for the extent of the build-up is significant and places the period of occupation at a minimum of several months.

Despite all the intervening years, the researchers were able to set foot on the floor where Knight himself once trod. The floor itself is clearly marked by a white layer of quartzite sand, 1–5 centimetres thick. Though roughly level, the floor drops abruptly by a number of centimetres in some locations, particularly around the outside walls. These breaks mark the location of additional internal structures or features such as door footings. Around the interior periphery of the foundation, and directly adjacent to the rock wall, are a number of wooden posts that supported the roof and wall, spaced 1.5 metres apart. Other post remnants were found in the central portion of the structure, adjacent to a collapsed brick hearth and chimney, which accounts for many of the 3500 bricks taken aboard the *Albany*. Despite the great interlude from the time they were built, the base remains 'laid in a Workman like manner wth Brick & Mortor'. The structure featured a central 'kitchen' area, also marked by the accumulation of hundreds of fragments of animal bone, leftovers from food preparation. This area is surrounded by sleeping quarters and narrow passageways. Shattered window glass was located adjacent to two exterior walls. The total surface area is approximately 250 square metres, and, with little room for comfort, could have accommodated forty men.

For more than two centuries there had been only speculation about the conditions in which the Knight expedition endured the Hudson Bay winter; now there was confirmation. While bearing little resemblance to such elaborate structures as York Fort, with its centrally located square house, enclosed by a palisade which linked four flankers or bastions, the design of

Knight's structure at Marble Island is consistent with at least some of those grandly styled 'fort' in the early history of the Hudson's Bay Company. It is impossible to reconcile the image of an inadequate shelter or 'mud hut', thrown together by a band of castaways, with that which was unearthed in August 1990, and further excavated twelve months later. Not only was its design and construction mindful of the region's harsh climate, but there is, considering the quantity of fuel consumed and the accumulation of detritus and soot, graphic evidence suggesting occupation of the site during the darkness of winter.

Still more remarkable than the existence of such a monumental early-eighteenth-century architectural undertaking in the Canadian tundra, and any conclusion about its length of occupancy, is the realization that it is a storehouse of artefacts lying much as Knight and his officers left them. What was unearthed by trowel and brush in the painstaking excavation conducted over the two field seasons was a series of artefacts, each more remarkable than the last. It was a glimpse of a world entirely different from our own, but more than that, valuable clues were found in the growing catalogue of miscellany to come from below the blanket of moss: five thousand objects of silver, brass, copper, iron, lead, wood, clay, leather, textiles, pottery, glass and, most important in terms of its historical implications, bone. In addition to removing any doubt about the age and origin of the site, artefact evidence took the investigation a step closer to the forgotten truth.

Relics were constantly being unearthed, but student field assistant Feliks Kappi, sifting the backdirt on a screen, surely the least glamorous task in what can be a singularly unglamorous occupation, made the first striking artefact discovery. 'A coin,' he announced, adding after a long pause, 'from 1644.' What can make one silver coin a treasure is the remarkable isolation of the place of its discovery. Soon other coins were recovered. To find silver and copper coinage from the first years of the eighteenth century on an island in Hudson Bay was nothing short of extraordinary. That money would have been carried into this region illustrates the depth of the belief that the expedition would succeed in reaching seas where it had value in trade.

Here, at least, it would have had no value at all. As curious are the places of origin. Of the copper coins, three, although badly corroded, appear to be English, though the date can be read on only one: 1700. A fourth, dated 1713, is Portuguese, showing the name of John V. The silver piece was also not English, as might have been expected, but Danish, bearing the likeness of King Christian IV. The reverse is marked 'Gluckstadt', a reference to the site, now in Germany, of the monarch's greatest military victory.

With several separate excavations underway at any one time, it was impossible to keep up with all the discoveries. It was only at the end of the day, when Beattie, who was buried in his own work of recording detailed level notes and keeping a photographic record of site profiles, entered the artefact tent and asked, 'What have I missed?', that the scope and significance of the discoveries became obvious. Among those laid out were a pair of the scissors mentioned on the expedition's list of trade goods, musket and pistol balls (one expended), decorative silver clasps, an amber button with a pastoral scene finely etched on its surface, buttons of filigreed metal, a blue and white china teapot lid, a small basket made of leather and wood, a lead weigh token, a barrel that once held gunpowder found crushed under a collapsed wall, and optical glass from a telescope. Not all were the possessions of expedition members. Two skilfully crafted Inuit instruments were also uncovered, a snow knife found in the disturbed layer above the floor, and a broken ivory leister, a pronged fish spear, found at floor level, directly associated with Knight relics.

However, the most haunting discovery was not an object that shed any light on the mystery, nor even one that would be readily associated with a voyage of discovery, but a wooden chess piece, a pawn. Somehow the piece represented a link between the world of today and those lost at this desolate place. In a chess match, the quickest win, called fool's mate, comes in four moves. Its occurrence usually results from the failure of one player to understand the rules of the game. A reminder of Knight's tragic miscalculation was made obvious by what lay near by, iron trusses and a large iron hinge, recalling that Knight 'was so confident of success, that he had strong chests made, bound with iron, to hold the gold and copper-ore'.

In one spectacular instance, the fragile remnants of a blue pouch, made of a stout hemp fabric, were discovered with the contents intact. Field assistant Yin Lam spent an entire day, 15 August 1991, hunched over the find, using a medical dissection probe and a soft-bristle brush to meticulously remove the dirt to expose and eventually retrieve its contents. Gradually revealed were a clay pipe, a wooden-handled iron corkscrew and a wooden reel around which was once coiled the line carrying a sounding lead. At one point Lam called out, 'I think we've got something here.' It was the most remarkable find of all, a pair of brass dividers, a nautical instrument used in charting a ship's location, perhaps the single most important relic of a Northwest Passage expedition to be found in the landscape of discovery since the nineteenth-century search for Franklin. Dividers have a history as long as the science of navigation, and are so conspicuous in the portraits of explorers, such as Sebastian Cabot, that they came to symbolize an entire age of exploration. At Marble Island, their discovery extended beyond symbolism to the realization of something both enchanting and troubling: that these were the possessions of an officer, perhaps Captains George Berley or David Vaughan, or perhaps even of Knight himself. It was grimly apparent that such an important instrument was not likely to have been easily lost or discarded.

Further clues, illustrating that a sizeable proportion of the expedition crewmen had occupied the site, were found in the fragmentary remnants of clothing, and the broad square toes and high wooden and layered leather heels of leather shoes that in 1767 had suggested to Master Joseph Stevens, 'ye appearance of French fashion'. That any clothing and footwear would have survived for nearly three centuries is in itself remarkable, and is due in part to the acidic conditions at the site. The ruin mimics a bog by retaining moisture during the brief summer months, and is then frozen for the remainder of the year, preserving fabric and leather against the destruction that would have otherwise been caused by chemical and physical factors and biological agents.

Through microscopic analysis at her laboratory at the Canadian Circumpolar Institute in Edmonton, Arctic textiles specialist Barb Schweger was able to determine that the preserved fabrics included wool, felt, bast fibres such as jute or hemp, and possibly linen. One large piece of red fabric was painted white on one side with a pigment of high lead content, and may represent cabin lining like that observed in the possession of the Inuit in 1722. Leather was also located, although its function could not be identified. Buttons did identify the origin of some of the fabric, which included remnants of shirts and heavy outer garments. In all, 97 buttons were collected (89 wood, 2 brass, 2 iron, 1 glass, 1 amber, 1 metal and wood, 1 wood with cloth cover). More significantly, through cleaning the footwear and comparison with rare existing examples from the early eighteenth century, Schweger was able to solve the centuries-old confusion over the shoes.

Thirty leather shoe soles and eleven heels were recovered. One shoe, despite its great age, was remarkably well preserved and resembled that which Stevens took 'to have been some officers'. It was not French fashion in the sense that Stevens

Brass dividers, a nautical instrument used in charting a ship's location, belonging to a member of the Knight expedition.

intended, concluding one of the mysterious vessels to have wintered at the site was French, and had 'gone well off'. Rather it represented what for a resident of London in 1719 would have been the height of fashion. The shoe was typical of those worn by gentlemen of the period and was at least the product of the influence of French style, namely rococo, then flourishing throughout western Europe. All that is missing is the metal buckle, an example of which was found nearby in the excavation. A second complete shoe was not so stylish, and by the coarseness of the workmanship suggested a more humble, if no more practical, owner. Directly associated with the shoe was twine made of horsehair. Neither of the two best-preserved examples of footwear was in any way well suited to the climate, and they probably represent summer or dress wear.

By a comparison of the different sizes of the soles and heels, it is estimated that the footwear represents an approximate minimum of fifteen of the expedition's forty men. Only two of the shoes did not conform to the general similarities of design. One was an unusual large wooden sole, which perhaps represented a form of snow boot bottom, and, most striking, a small (size 5), narrow shoe with a fancy metal buckle. The height of its owner would not have exceeded 1.25 metres, strong evidence that a boy was taken on the expedition. Boy apprentices as young as twelve, usually wards of Christ's Hospital, London, referred to as 'bluecoat boys', were indentured into the Hudson's Bay Company's service for tours of duty in the northern wilderness lasting as long as seven years. Ultimately the quantity and variety of the garments and footwear demonstrates that many of the expedition crewmen occupied the site, and tells something of them, although it does not provide any special insight into their fate. What survives may well be items passed over or missed under collapsed walls by natives who availed themselves of expedition effects after the deaths of its members, or it might as likely represent only what was abandoned by expedition members as superfluous.

What was certainly discarded without thought was a great quantity of empty bottles. Some of the glass was from small and fragile medicine bottles, although evidence of drink abounds in innumerable broken bottles of olive-green glass with a long neck and a deep kick, characteristic of the early eighteenth century. In all, 755 fragments were found littering the area around and inside the house, including nine bottoms and twenty corks. Apparently wine bottles – though Knight saw to it that the ships also carried a bounty of brandy, spirits and strong beer – only two remain largely intact, one corked and containing a residue of the original contents. The bouquet, however, was that of mouldering vegetation. The expedition carried spirits alone to last a full year, with the bulk of the refreshments stored aboard the *Albany*, bringing to mind the assurance Knight had once given that 'no Man can brann me a Drunken Governr'. While his personal preference was for snuff, Knight had once complained of being made an 'Absolute Smoker', and there remains ample evidence of smoking among Knight's crews, namely the abundance of stem and bowl fragments from broken clay pipes, some still containing tobacco.

Fundamental questions about the fate of the expedition remained to be answered, and in that context the most valuable information was drawn from the least valuable of the artefacts: the food refuse. During the excavations, discarded animal bone was found concentrated in the food preparation area within the structure, as well as in the 41-metre-square test pits dug randomly in the environs of the ruin. In excess of six hundred

Gentleman's shoe unearthed from within the ruin of
Knight's shelter, the kind that first suggested 'French fashion'.

bones or bone fragments were recovered, two-thirds of which are identifiable by species. The argument frequently used in support of Hearne's theory of 'sickness and famine' is that the provisions taken on the voyage were inadequate, and that Knight tragically miscalculated the ability of the crews to obtain sufficient supplies of fresh meat at such a high latitude. These conclusions, based in equal measure on Company account books which contain provisioning information, and on assumption, can be finally confronted through scrutiny of the provision lists, coupled with analysis of the actual food refuse found at the site.

Insight into the expedition supplies is gleaned by comparing what was taken by Knight aboard the *Albany* and the *Discovery* with that carried by the two Company supply frigates, the *Hudson's Bay* and the *Mary*, which departed the same day for their yearly, six-month round trip to the Company's outposts in Hudson and James bays. Though no surviving documents list precise crew sizes for the *Albany* and the *Discovery*, it is possible to establish an accurate estimate by comparison with the *Hudson's Bay* and the *Mary*. Committee Minute Book records show that the officers and men aboard the two supply frigates totalled forty-three, and that wages paid to these crews

Neck of broken wine bottle, one of numerous examples
strewn over the wintering site.

amounted to £188. Also recorded for the same pay period are the wages for the *Albany* and the *Discovery*, an amount of £110. Therefore, assuming the wages to be relatively constant between the four ships, the number of officers and crew aboard the *Albany* and the *Discovery* would have been approximately twenty-six. In addition, the expedition carried ten 'landsmen passengers', paid separately, Knight himself, his two commanders and an individual paid a gratuity along with Knight, presumably charged with overseeing the mining endeavours. This gives an estimated forty men on the expedition: probably twenty-eight aboard the *Albany* and twelve aboard the tiny sloop *Discovery*. These expedition numbers and the victualling records allow extrapolation of the length of time the food provisions would have been expected to last. The discovery expedition carried enough beef, pork, bacon, 'stock fish', bread, flour, butter, 'groceries' and other provisions to last a minimum of nine and a half months.

Examination of the individual items and types of foods provides additional valuable information. All of the foodstuffs supplied, such staples as flour, bread and 'groceries', which typically included everything from casks of peas to prunes, would probably have been the least variable between the discovery and supply voyages, and therefore provide the most reliable estimate of how long the provisions would have lasted. A comparison of the quantities taken indicates that the *Albany* and the *Discovery* were provisioned for nine and a half months. By contrast, other items vary dramatically between the discovery ships and the supply ships plying their annual course to Hudson Bay and back. For example, butter, bacon and chops were supplied in a quantity to last Knight's expedition fourteen months. Beef and pork on the other hand would only have lasted the expedition about four months and fish six and a half. This was augmented by large quantities of 'junk', salt meat used as food on long voyages which, the common complaint was, had the consistency of rope. Unlike the supply ships, it is clear that the crews of the *Albany* and the *Discovery* also planned to supplement their animal protein with fresh meat, and to that end were carrying a fourteen-month supply of salt with which to preserve the catch. To assist in the hunt the expedition was heavily armed with fifty pieces and sixteen barrels of gunpowder.

Given that a large portion of the bone found was strewn around on the surface outside the ruin, generally in association with other expedition artefacts such as pipe stems, nails or bottle glass, and that less than five per cent of the site's surface area was excavated by removing the overlying moss layer, it was concluded the bone and bone fragments discovered represent only a small portion of the animal protein available to, and consumed by, expedition members. Still, the remains include a mix of species brought from England, as well as a diversity of local species. From the random cross-section of bone collected, it is evident that the expedition succeeded in obtaining fresh meat, either through hunting or trade, as only approximately one-third of the bone present represents domesticated animals, including cow, pig, sheep and poultry, as well as 'stock fish' – cod or halibut. By contrast, the remainder of the animal protein in the diet consisted of hunted foods, including caribou, ptarmigan, snow goose, eider duck, ringed seal, beluga whale, polar bear, Arctic hare and Arctic char. Knife marks and saw marks on twenty-one of the bones of both domestic and hunted animals confirm that they were butchered by Knight's men, or, in the case of the domestic animals, butchered in England in preparation for the voyage. Five of the bones are carbonized, indicating some degree of cooking or burning on an open flame, while another six are calcined (transformed to a porcelain white consistency), indicating that they have been burned for some time in an intense fire.

The faunal remains of hunted species represent only a portion of possible food sources for the expedition; extending the excavation area would have certainly revealed others. Since evidence of supplemental food sources, flour and other perishables, is not available, a definitive inventory of all food consumed at the site is not possible. The evidence demonstrates, however, that Knight clearly understood the implications of failing to provide adequate supplies for the winter in such a climate. Not only do his entries in the 1717

Churchill Journal evoke the lesson of Munk's disastrous winter at the Churchill River, but they reveal a basic understanding of the function of antiscorbutics in warding off scurvy. At one point he writes, 'here is not Garden Stuff nor fresh Meat to be had to purge & Sweeten the Blood'. Quantities of both lemon juice and rhubarb, effective against scurvy, were commonly supplied to Company forts during Knight's governorship, and almost certainly featured prominently among the large supply of groceries and medicine taken on the voyage.

The possibility that the expedition simply did not have enough fresh provisions to feed its forty members throughout a single winter cannot be ruled out, though the evidence at the site strongly indicates that it is more reasonable to conclude otherwise. It is difficult to see how this finding can comfortably fit with the sorrowful description given Hearne of the diminished numbers of expedition survivors who shambled out from their house at the end of that first winter to lengthen their longboat.

The last clue was potentially the most definitive. It was in an area directly adjacent to the fallen form of Knight's structure that the initial discovery came, found in one of the first test pits excavated. Bill Gawor, archaeological field assistant Martin Amy and David Tatuiini, an Inuk student assistant from Rankin Inlet, crouched over the excavation. With each fistful of moss, they began the routine of pulling against the roots of dwarf willows that anchored the vegetation. When the roots finally gave way, they sifted through the exposed ground with the tips of their trowels, searching for artefacts. Pieces of glass and clay pipe were found, as well as fragments of animal bone. At first no one noticed the small object that clung under the root mat that had just been removed. Earlier, during the foot survey, Tatuiini had viewed with evident bemusement the importance assigned to each brick and broken clay pipe found. This time, his interest piqued, he leaned closer and then pointed to it with his trowel. 'Is it bone?' he murmured, more to himself than the others. Work on the excavation continued. When bone had been found before, it was that of seal, ptarmigan or caribou, often with the tell-tale signs of butchering, evidence that Knight's crews had obtained, through hunting or trading, fresh provisions. But this tiny bone was different. Beattie inspected it for some time, and then once again when he returned to his university laboratory in Edmonton. Some of the anatomical detail on the surface of the lumbar vertebra had been destroyed by the acidity of the soil, but enough remained. It was human.

After the passage of nearly three centuries, human remains endured at the site, and in and about the very location Hearne had described sighting them, 'lying above-ground close to the house'. The potential represented by that one small bone was great. That single vertebra might have been a crucial memory of a distant disaster, a time before the long lapse into the unknown. Perhaps even, as Hearne argued, it represented the remains of one of the last survivors, even the last man, the armourer or smith, lying today in the very place where he had fallen, 'in attempting to dig a grave for his companion'. It was only a fragment, yet its significance came from being one element of Hearne's account of the human toll of the disaster to be matched by the archaeology.

Excavations of the site adjacent to the vertebra and further upslope failed to yield any additional human bone, only frustration. One small bone is not enough to judge any-thing conclusively. It could simply have been an aberration, bone from Inuit or Thule graves on the island, scattered by scavenging animals, not unlike the human bone on the surface in the area of Inuit occupation across the harbour from the expedition ruin. Nonetheless, in archaeological and forensic investigations, even such a seemingly minor clue can be of critical importance when taken together with other evidence. Certainly, animals had gnawed on the vertebra, for the porous and nutrient-filled body was gone, leaving behind only the vertebra arch, bone responsible for protecting the spinal cord. However, key information about the individual represented by the remains was obtained through lead-isotope analysis, a means of 'fingerprinting' trace lead content in bone to establish its place of origin. In this case it was confirmed that the spine fragment represented remains of an Englishman, or, at the very least, someone who had spent a considerable time in England.

The only other human remains came from within the ruin, first one tooth, a maxillary right first molar, from a young man. There were tobacco stains ringing the crown, indicating that it was not from an Inuk, but from one of Knight's men. The tooth was found in an area that had suffered disturbance, and was in proximity to a shoe sole, at a level 15–20 centimetres above the original floor. The amount of wear on the surface of the tooth revealed the man was probably in his twenties. Soon, when the excavation reached floor level, other teeth were uncovered, a maxillary right third molar and a mandibular right second molar from one individual. Once again, tobacco stains on the enamel, and the general dimensions and characteristics of the teeth, indicated that they belonged most likely to a Caucasoid individual.

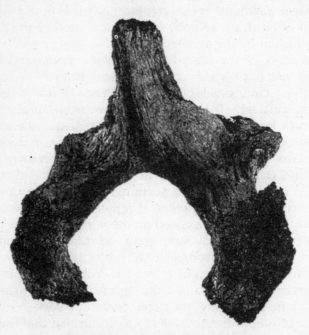

Human vertebral arch.

It is remotely possible that the teeth were lost as a result of scurvy. This serious Vitamin C deficiency disease is known to result in bleeding gums and loosening teeth, with occasional tooth loss. However, this would most likely have resulted in the loss of the single rooted teeth at the front of the jaws like incisors or canines, its incidence being rare for multi-rooted teeth like molars. In this case tooth loss may also be attributed to a forceful blow to the right side of the face, either accidental or in violence. The most likely explanation, however, is that the teeth were dislodged after the individual's death, perhaps by a hatchet or shovel used in the search for 'any thing remarkable, such as papers', a search that instead unearthed a human skull which was then taken away. There was, however, no accompanying bone, nor anything to indicate the presence of a body.

Physical evidence supports the accounts of the first Europeans to examine the site of the disaster and their evidence for the existence of the remains of several bodies on the surface. First, the context of the three teeth located in the structure during the 1990 excavation had served to corroborate Master Joseph Stevens and Master Magnus Johnston in their account of the discovery of a human skull unearthed while digging for papers inside the foundation. Stevens recorded that it was found at floor level 'abt 3 feet down', and Johnston mentions that it was found in proximity to 'severall English mens shoes', indicating the remains had lain on the floor while the structure was still standing. Physical evidence had also been found in support of Hearne's observation that 'sculls and other large bones' of Knight expedition crewmen were 'now lying above-ground close to the house'. Together, they provide physical evidence to support historical claims that the island's barren surface was indeed the final resting-place for at least three of the 'Unhappey Sufferars', those whose deaths have for centuries raised a chill of horror among all those to have contemplated Captain James Knight's destruction while searching for the illusory Strait of Anian and its mineral splendour. Yet the archaeological investigation raised the spectre of something with more profound implications for the investigation of Knight's disappearance.

There was no single point of realization that Hearne's pitiable depiction of the end of the Knight expedition was fundamentally at odds with the surviving physical record, especially since the surface remains were consistent, not with the second-hand account of a 'great Number of graves' attributed to Hearne, but with his own published account of the bones of the last survivors. Instead a growing acceptance was arising from the collating of the evidence. The presence of physical evidence that Knight's crews had an adequate food supply, including freshly caught meat, for one winter, observations regarding the elaborate precautions made in response to the severe climate in the design and construction of the shelter, and the compelling case for the occupation of the site during the depths of winter, suggest a very different conclusion from that offered by Hearne. Under such circumstances, even with an expedition graveyard, it would be hard to consider it a reasonable possibility that the numbers of crewmen could have been 'greatly reduced' by starvation and scurvy that first winter.

Tooth showing tobacco stains.

10

The PHANTOM SHIP

It was finally left to the vanished ships. Tradition has it that Marble Island was formed of ice, but there is another, subterranean, element to the legend. A great chasm in the ice was filled with sea water, creating a harbour, believed to be bottomless. The deep has since proven to be something less than that, as submerged only a few fathoms below the grey waves lay the graveyard of one, purportedly two, discovery vessels from the early years of the eighteenth century. There existed clues vital to any reconsideration of the last hours or last days of the *Albany* and the *Discovery*, and whatever else could be known of the expedition's fate.

An underwater search for the wrecks had been a theoretical possibility, but the need had never been anticipated. It was only in 1991, when armed with evidence that Knight's crews had the provisions necessary for wintering, that Beattie realized fully the significance of Hearne's telling of the ship and sloop. They represented the last line of physical evidence, and it somehow seemed only fitting. For as much as it was the desire and enterprise of Captains James Knight, George Berley and David Vaughan, or the strength and seamanship of their crews, the spirit of discovery was propelled by its sails, not great ships, slow and ungainly, but lighter and simpler vessels. The *Albany* had already ridden the cold currents of Hudson Bay. The *Discovery* was on her maiden voyage, like her namesake, Henry Hudson's *Discovery*, seeking a passage to the western ocean. In his *Journey* Hearne recounted seeing 'the hulls, or more properly speaking, the bottoms of the ship and sloop, which lie sunk in about five fathoms of water, toward the head of the harbour'. Their murky sleep has been virtually undisturbed. Free of the destructive action of woodborers, and protected from the grinding force of the ice along the exposed coast, the cove's frigid calm would have left them largely unchanged in all the intervening years.

The very reason James Knight went to Marble Island in 1719 is judged to be among the most baffling mysteries related to the expedition's destruction. Just a year earlier Knight was laid out with illness and it has been generally supposed that given his great age and recent medical history, there would be some reasonable doubt that he could have survived another Arctic winter. In the gruesome relics of Jens Munk's expedition Knight had likewise seen firsthand the grim toll of unpreparedness on an expedition's crews. These observations fit the earliest references to the expedition's disappearance, which attributed the cause of the disaster not to Knight's resolve in attaining his treasure, but to misadventure, the belief that the *Albany* and the *Discovery* were shipwrecked, perhaps driven ashore by storm, on their arrival at Marble Island. This is the representation given to Moses Norton in 1765 by the two Inuit boys, repeating what they had been told by their elders, 'that ye 2 Vessels was lost in ye fall of ye year about Marble Island but ye Crews got safe ashore'. Similarly, Hearne's intelligence revealed that the vessels had arrived at Marble Island late in the autumn, with the largest ship suffering serious damage 'in getting them into the harbour'.

Yet neither account can be easily reconciled with what existed on the island, for evidently it was not only the crews that 'got safe ashore'. Whatever damage the *Albany* in particular may have suffered, it had not prevented the offloading of tons of bricks, the vast stores of provisions, the house in frame and the chaldrons of coal carried in the hold of the frigate. It is possible that the damaged vessels were driven into the shallow water near the head of the cove, and their cargoes retrieved in that manner. However, the detailed journal entry scrawled by Master Joseph Stevens on 23 July 1767 provides compelling evidence that, forty-eight years earlier, the *Albany* and the *Discovery* arrived without serious incident. Stevens describes discovering three anchors on shore above the tide, but what is significant is the presence of hawsers, worn through by chafing on the ice. According to the master, one '10¼ inch cable' remained in good condition 'tho Rubed through in several places as I judge by ye Ice when ye Ship was moored Like Wise several Peaces of Towlines &c in same Condition'. A critical evaluation of this conclusion, that the vessel or vessels were 'moored', suggests that it is just as reasonable to view the circumstances of the expedition's entry of the harbour not as an image of devastation, the first event in a ever-compounding saga of misfortune, but somewhat less dramatically, as a logical winter quarters safely gained.

The expedition must have spent August and September 1719 feeling its way along the coast for the passage that would take them away from the darkening skies, before finally turning to Marble Island. Knight was almost certainly aware of the existence of the island's cove through *North-West Fox*, the published narrative of Captain Luke Foxe, who recorded in 1631, 'there is a Cove or Harbour, made by small islands,

Exploration in Hudson Bay, taken from Henry Ellis's account of the 1746–7 voyage by the *Dobbs Galley* and the *California*.

141

that a ship may ride in safety, for all weathers, and have two fathomes at low water; it is on the Eastside'. What is more, Foxe also reported plentiful waterfowl and the possibility 'that there was store of Deere in that Island'. Even the white stone seemed to lend itself to practical uses: 'I take it to be such as they pave their houses with in Holland.' It is difficult today to understand how the cove could ever have been judged adequate for a ship to ride in safely, for even at high tide the water at either cove entrance reaches a depth of only a metre, a seemingly impossible barrier even for the *Albany*, a frigate of small draught especially designed to enter the shallow Albany River, or for the diminutive *Discovery*. But in 1767, Stevens concluded it would be possible for a vessel to enter 'at high water'.

In a sense these are not the islands that either Knight or, forty-eight years later, Stevens visited. Geologically, the islands are in flux. During the last great ice age, immense layers of ice weighed down the floor of what is now Hudson Bay. With the retreat of the ice and the lifting of this oppressive weight, the land began to rebound. This process, called isostatic rebound, has been underway for 10,000 years, and is responsible for the very creation of Marble and Quartzite Islands. Today the rebound is still occurring at a rate of nearly one metre a century. Even over the geologically insignificant period of time since Knight and his men walked on this ground, the islands have risen over two metres. Most importantly, the resulting drop in the high-tide level has dramatically altered the characteristics of the harbour where Knight's ships sought shelter. If, in 1719, the islands appeared as they are today, it would have been impossible for the ships to have even entered the harbour and Marble Island would have perhaps been passed by. In many respects it was that marginal harbour that enticed the expedition into perilous circumstances.

There may have been 'great reason to think a ship has ben lost here', but adding to the puzzle is evidence detailed by Stevens during his reconnaissance, observations not simply of wreckage but of the systematic dismantling of one or more vessels for their raw material. On the nearby smooth rock face, there were, among a large quantity of wood chips, recognizable fragments of a ship's hull, including part of a channel-wale, timbers fastened to the side of the hull at or above the water-line. Stevens credited the work to carpenters, although at least some was judged to be 'natives Works'. Hearne, who visited the scene within days of Stevens, is more adamant, declaring the woodwork the product of work undertaken by Knight's crews, a view consistent with his interpretation that after the first winter, expedition survivors:

> were then very busily employed, but about what they could not easily describe, probably in lengthening the long-boat; for at a little distance from the house there is now lying a great quantity of oak chips, which have been most assuredly made by carpenters.

Stevens's account of the extent to which the vessels had been disassembled, including 'peaces of her Carve Work' and 'ye Stepes of her Side Port', even the broken stems and removal of the rings from the anchors by either 'ye Natives or them Selves', would suggest an undertaking far more ambitious than the lengthening of a longboat. It is doubtful such an effort would even have been required given both that the numbers of the English were purportedly 'greatly reduced' after the first winter, and that the Knight expedition was equipped to engage in whaling and would probably have carried enough small boats with which the survivors could have made good an escape. Company documents show that even the sloop *Discovery* was equipped with her own boat.

The goal was now to probe beneath the surface of the cove and establish the presence and condition of Knight's two discovery vessels. The only evidence of either located during the land-based archaeology was a stanchion, a vertical structure that once supported a deck. Still, much more was already known to exist. In 1971 a team of divers had established in part the accuracy of Hearne's description by relocating at the head of the harbour the *Albany*, although a thermocline, a sudden variation in water temperature, limited visibility to 'a

143

clutch of wooden shapes protruding out of the cloudy silt'. By touch, the divers determined the presence of a vessel measuring approximately 20 metres, lying on its side with its stern about 15 metres from the cove's south-east shore. The dimensions suggested it was the larger of the two, the 80-ton *Albany*. Left unknown was the nature and degree of the damage done to the *Albany*, and just as significantly, confirmation of the presence of the *Discovery* and the source of any damage done to her. Captain David Vaughan had been issued orders to 'take Especiall Care to Return Back before you are in Danger of being frozen up', but only in the event of the sloop's separation from the larger vessel, which carried the bulk of the provisions necessary for wintering in the grim climate. The *Discovery* posed a particular problem for Hearne, who failed to reconcile the presence of a second submerged hull with the absence of an account from his informants regarding any damage done on the sloop's entry to the harbour. It posed a problem for the latest research too, for the absence of the *Discovery* had the potential to alter fundamentally any interpretation of the disaster.

Joining the project to assist in the underwater survey conducted in 1991 and 1992 were Andy Cameron, a researcher with the USA's National Aeronautics and Space Administration, who served as technical adviser. Don Palfrey, an experienced Arctic diver, served as lead diver, while Jeff Gilmour assisted as project diver. Among his qualifications, Palfrey boasts the rank of commodore of the only slightly whimsical Rankin Inlet Yacht Club, an organization without a fleet but with an impressive record of community service. Together, the three additions to the crew contributed to the awakening of additional knowledge, long-lost intimations of the fate of the Knight expedition.

The technical nature of the underwater archaeological survey belied its purpose: the location of two vessels locked for centuries in their frigid stupor, and the human tragedy their presence would represent. The icy grey waters themselves seemed to dull realization of the significance of human history represented there, its toneless qualities better reflecting the monotony of establishing a sonar grid by repeated crossings of the cove in a small launch. When the sonar passes were made along the grid lines, and anomalies in the form of unusual bottom features were detected, these were then investigated by the divers. Incredibly, no sonar was needed in 1991 to locate the phantom form of the *Albany*. While restricted visibility underwater created the sensation of diving into heavy clouds, Palfrey emerged to report he had not first seen the ship, but 'hit it with my knee'. His subsequent investigations disturbed the silt suspended in the water enough to disperse it; the underwater fog had lifted. There, seen at a depth of 4–5 metres from the boat above, was James Knight's flagship, the *Albany*.

It was almost imperceptible at first. Staring down into the cove, Beattie saw only wraithlike tendrils of organic material reaching up from the murk, slowly undulating in the sluggish current. Then large, irregular shapes began to take form as his eyes were drawn deeper by the filaments. Finally, darker, angular objects projecting from the olive-green bottom just at the edge of vision identified the skeleton of a ship. The hull, consistent with that of an 80-ton frigate, was resting on its port side, running nearly perpendicular to the south shore of the harbour, where a natural quay is formed by the stone. The stern is nearest to the south-east limit of the cove, the bow once pointing into the prevailing north-westerly wind, possible further evidence of the navigable condition of the ship since it would have been brought about to assume this position.

Amazingly, despite the gulf of time from its sinking, the hull of Knight's flagship remains largely intact, separated into two in-line sections. It was impossible, in a non-invasive assessment, to determine the exact cause of the breakage, although there was no tear or gash evident to suggest that damage to the hull was inflicted by some catastrophic occurrence, such as being driven up on rocks or shoals. There may have been damage inflicted as the vessel entered the harbour, but in no way does it give the appearance of having foundered or that they would have had to offload in haste. Rather, the appearance is of separation after the *Albany* had settled on the bottom. What is immediately apparent is the degree to which the vessel had been cannibalized for materials. Most evidence of the raised quarterdeck and forecastle are gone, and some of the mid-deck planking has been removed. On the starboard side, ribs protrude above where planks were also removed, creating an eerie, skeletal air.

The problem of the *Discovery* remained. Compounding the difficulties confronted when the underwater survey was extended in 1992 in search of the *Discovery* was a deterioration in conditions. Extreme cold above the water, at times with rain sluicing down, and poor visibility below, hampered the effort. Repeated sonar passes failed to identify anything that resembled the missing sloop either towards the head of the harbour, or farther off. After several days of a futile search the team was confronted with the real possibility that the *Discovery* was not there, a conclusion that would have only further confounded the Knight expedition mystery. Then, while making one sonar pass, several anomalies were noted to the south-west of the *Albany*, distant from its superstructure or any associated debris. Zero visibility was typical, and the divers relied solely on physical touch to explore the features. In describing the conditions, Palfrey likened it to 'going along a banister with the lights off'.

Despite the difficulties, Palfrey and Gilmour, working in depths of 3–4.5 metres, located two in-line, square hardwood ribs rising near vertically from the bottom. The top of the ribs, measuring about 10 centimetres square, appeared to have been sheared off, perhaps by ice, with the bottom portions connected by planking and disappearing into the silty bottom. On the second day sonar identified two additional ribs, in-line with the other, all evenly spaced. The planking and ribs seemed to follow a slight arc, consistent with the hull of a small-to-medium-size vessel, the size of the *Discovery*. Soon Gilmour came across a 'stump' 45 centimetres in diameter and protruding 60 centimetres from the mud and silt on the floor of the cove. From its size, and configuration in relation to the ribs, it was almost certainly the base of a mast, and was fixed to a much larger structure buried in the silt. The weather was deteriorating rapidly in August 1992, preventing additional exploration of the new discovery. Further underwater archaeological investigation is required to identify definitively the wreckage and fully assess its condition. Even so its location and context leave little doubt that it is the elusive *Discovery*. Considering the orientation of the *Albany*, the mooring configuration of the sloop with the bow towards shore would have been consistent with the period. When beam to beam with another ship the bows typically face into the prevailing wind; when moored alongside a larger vessel the position is often reversed with the sloop on the lea side bow to stern.

Not only that: the *Discovery*, like the *Albany*, had been used as a source of raw materials. When the divers placed their masks against the top of the mast stump, they could see it had the appearance of having been 'chiselled', bringing to mind the recovery by Master John Scroggs in 1722 of the lower part of a ship's foremast, 'broke off about five Foot above the deck', in the waters near Marble Island. Later, in July of that year, Scroggs searched for further signs, stumbling on an Inuit camp on the island, where he found, among other things, cabin lining, and ships' spars which had been 'split into Tent Poles, and Tents covered with Sails'. Through the centuries of European exploration in the Arctic there were but few events that generated great concentrations of what were, for the people of the region, a treasure of rare and exotic materials, and these inevitably resulted from abandoned ships and shipwrecks.

One of these incidents occurred in 1853, with the abandon-ment of the Franklin search ship HMS *Investigator* at Mercy Bay on north-eastern Banks Island. Resource extraction and distri-bution resulted in drastic changes to the lives of the Copper Inuit of the western Arctic. Suddenly they were made 'wealthy' by control of vast quantities of raw materials that were used for their own utilitarian and decorative purposes, for gift-giving or as valuable trade commodities. The Inuit who claimed the material sources, and those with whom they interacted and traded, were greatly affected culturally and socially for decades, until the materials were distributed far afield and the sources dried up. The *Albany* and the *Discovery* proved as rich a bounty. As is starkly illustrated by Scroggs's testimony, the materials offloaded by the crews, the construction materials and contents of the house, and the ships themselves, would have had an impact on the lives of the people of the region for years, even decades, after all expedition members were dead. How then, nearly half a century after the fact, Hearne could conclude that the oak chips were 'most assuredly made by carpenters' is unknown.

While the accuracy of Hearne's assessment of the sunken vessels is confirmed not only by his description of their location near the head of the harbour, but also by his choice of wording in reference to 'the hulls, or more properly speaking, the bottoms of the ship and sloop', it is his interpretations regarding the source of the damage that are critically flawed. There is no evidence today to support the theory that expedition crews were salvaging planks to fashion an escape vessel, nor does it appear they would have had cause. There was something frightful, inexorable, in the realization, after four seasons of meticulous, sometimes exasperating, research into the disappearance of the Knight expedition, that not only does there appear to have been adequate provisions for forty men to have lasted the winter, but that one, perhaps two, serviceable vessels were abandoned while moored.

11

A GOTHIC JOURNEY

Hearne tells of the destruction of the Knight expedition with such a direct simplicity, and his own recollections and those of his informants are presented with such conviction, that for more than two centuries they assumed the lustre of reality. Not only was there cause to believe in his portrayal, but there was a compelling desire to. His picturesque depiction of the last two survivors provided an image of dauntless courage in the face of untold peril, perseverance against all hope. A Victorian etching shows the tattered last survivors, one with his head cupped in his hands, the other refusing to surrender faith, but below them is the written assurance, 'No hope!'. Frederick Whymper concludes his stirring 1875 account, *Heroes of the Arctic*, with a stern lecture to a generation of English schoolboys about 'seriousness in the conduct of life'. It is not the only lesson provided by Hearne's skilful reconstruction of the Knight disaster. There are few accounts better designed to reinforce the folly of the basis on which, and the manner in which, Knight chose to conquer the northern landscape.

Hearne's strength lies in the advantage of having received his detailed account from the people of the region, people, presumably, with a collective knowledge of the fate of Knight. Inuit testimony, such as that on the fate of Sir John Franklin obtained by Dr John Rae while surveying the Boothia Peninsula in 1854, has proven an invaluable, usually accurate source of information. Yet historical questions have occasionally arisen regarding Hearne's account, such as the interpretation of the

historian Arthur S. Morton that attempts to reconcile it with
Scroggs. Hearne's depiction of most deaths was accurate, it is
argued, save for the last few survivors, who were probably
polished off by Inuit anxious to get at the wealth of iron and
wood. Morton's theory judges the last survivor, according to
Hearne probably 'the armourer, or smith', as evidence that
a few Knight expedition survivors, such as the blacksmith,
may have been spared for a time to fashion implements for
the victors. Responsibility for any perceived inaccuracies in
Hearne's account, however, invariably rests with what he had
been told by his Inuit informants, who 'may be excused for
picturing their fierce countrymen in the part of benefactors' –
never with Hearne himself.

The common assumption is that Hearne was simply acting
in the capacity of a stenographer when he evoked the vivid
image of the tragedy at Marble Island in the introduction to
*A Journey From Prince of Wales's Fort in Hudson's Bay To The
Northern Ocean*, an acknowledged masterpiece among early
journals and narratives. This may well be the case, except
that there remains the problem of the discrepancy between the
contents of Hearne's introduction and the key omission in the
logbooks of the sloop masters at Marble Island in 1769, which
fail to make any reference to there finally being a resolution of
the mysterious loss of the expedition. In 1767 Magnus Johnston
questioned area Inuit but concluded as to their fate, 'I cannot
find out As yet.'

Joseph Stevens, who devoted pages of his ship's journal to an
exhaustive description of the site after its discovery, and who
described the location of relics again the following year, is mute
on the matter of a proposed solution. Nor is there any record
that Hearne himself, a conscientious and ambitious Company
servant, ever bothered to inform any of his superiors of this
intelligence, including Moses Norton, chief factor at Prince
of Wales's Fort, whose interest in the fate of the Knight
expedition is evident from his own journal. There are some
things we can never know. Not least baffling among the many
mysteries shrouding the Knight expedition is the long and
unexplained pause before Samuel Hearne shared his account

of the disaster. Hearne in fact did not record the scene until more than two decades later, when the introduction to his *Journey* was completed in 1790.

Hearne's celebrated overland treks across the Barren Lands to the northern ocean, undertaken in 1769–73, were descended of Knight's own search. Indian reports of the distant copper mines did not die with Knight. Those who succeeded him in the government of Hudson Bay, James Isham and Moses Norton, were also lured by the stories of mineral treasure, Isham enquiring in the 1740s how many 'moon's itt wou'd take an English man to go'. In 1762 Norton himself set out in search of the Northwest Passage, the successful navigation of which was still held to be the only means of obtaining the mineral riches. His hopes were temporarily dashed when he steered a cutter into not the legendary passage, but Baker Lake. But he persisted, later sending two Indians, Matonabbee and Idotlyazee, to trace to their source 'ye largest Rivers to ye Northward'. The two returned after several years carrying copper samples and 'a Draught of ye Coast' depicting the

Samuel Hearne's view of Prince of Wales's Fort.

151

location of the copper mines. It was on the basis of this evidence that Norton enticed the Company to once again authorize an expedition for discovery of the copper mines and the Northwest Passage. The tenets of this expedition, however, could scarcely have been more different from those which had failed Knight.

Samuel Hearne, who had just returned with the whaling sloops from his final stop at Marble Island, was selected by Norton in 1769 to undertake an overland journey to the distant river believed to 'abound with copper ore'. Hearne was entrusted in this great and onerous undertaking to the care of a Chipewyan conjurer, or medicine man, who had personally never seen the mineral riches, and whose particular talents appear to have been expended rather in conjuring up ways to relieve Hearne of his possessions. Hearne left Prince of Wales's Fort in November 1769 to a seven-gun salute, but within a month had staggered back to the post. Surprised by the expedition's hasty reappearance, Norton began to organize another attempt, although this time the send-off was limited to three cheers. The second journey also ended ingloriously, with Hearne at one point concluding that 'they were entirely loste'. Finally on his third attempt, after a bitter, albeit justified, falling out with Norton over selection of personnel, Hearne this time joined the company of the Chipewyan leader Matonabbee.

It was under the direction of Matonabbee, to whom Hearne attributed abilities and a character that 'could not be exceeded by the most illustrious personage now on record', and by the adoption of the living ways of his fellow travellers, that Hearne walked across the vast Barren Lands, witnessing acts of great and wanton cruelty, suffering enormous personal hardship and privation, all the while mapping and describing a wilderness much of which was not visited by a white man again until the twentieth century. His *Journey* is alive with strange life and phenomena. He describes witnessing frozen frogs, wrapped in warm skins and exposed to a slow fire, recover life. He wondered at others who had observed aurora borealis without mentioning what accompanied their visual splendour, the 'rustling and crackling noise, like the waving of a large flag in a fresh gale of wind'. He made record of the customs, the spirituality of the aboriginal peoples he encountered, all the while moving farther away from his own world, to the Coppermine River, the shore of the northern ocean, and finally to the fabled copper mines.

Half a century after Knight's death, a European had finally reached mines that Hearne reports the Indians had represented to be 'so rich and valuable, that if a factory were built at the river, a ship might be ballasted with the ore, instead of stone'. Perhaps because this account differed so much from what he actually encountered, the resulting geological reconnaissance undertaken by Hearne and his companions fell somewhat short of being exhaustive. They devoted less than four hours to the actual search for copper and Hearne less than a page of his journal to a discussion of the subject. It is perhaps a tribute to the intellectual qualities of Hearne's journey that while the object of his search, the copper mines, is passed over, his journal allots nearly as much text to a consideration of the beliefs of his Indian companions, who 'imagine that every bit of copper they find resembles some object in nature', such as a hare.

Hearne's slender treatment of the copper mines in his account is indicative, at least, of what he found. He had been told the 'hills were entirely composed of that metal, all in handy lumps, like a heap of pebbles'. In fact, if the expedition's geographical accomplishments were singular, so was the resulting mineral haul – a single sample of any importance was recovered, and it weighed less than 2 kilograms. There was native copper in unknown quantities, but Hearne's greatest accomplishment in prospecting was to demonstrate that any mining endeavour would prove uneconomical given the great distances involved. Returning to Prince of Wales's Fort in June 1772, he completed a remarkable two-year trek into the depths of the continent, one that ranks among the greatest exploits of northern discovery.

Despite its meagre pay-off, the Company rewarded Hearne in 1775 with command of the post Knight had founded, England's most northerly outpost in America, Prince of Wales's Fort. By its very isolation, the fort appeared safe from the War of Independence, the conflagration that at the same time engulfed American colonies at lower latitudes. Even if rebels had turned up at its gates, Prince of Wales's Fort had the menacing appearance of invincibility, its massive stone battlements surmounted with forty guns. It was not the rebel colonists who arrived in Hudson Bay, however, but their French allies, who retained more than just a passing interest in the region. In August 1782 the Comte de la Pérouse brought a formidable French flotilla within range of the fort. After landing troops and preparing for the bombardment, La Pérouse demanded the fur traders' surrender. Finding his position indefensible despite the appearances, Hearne hastily worked out the terms of surrender. This time Hearne was not relieved of any personal belongings, save the manuscript of his *Journey*, but of his charge, Prince of Wales's Fort.

The English fur traders were taken prisoner and the stone fortress destroyed by the French as part of a design to inflict economic hardship on English holdings. The fate of the manuscript was another matter. La Pérouse seized it with the notion that it was Company property and as such, belonged among the spoils of war. On studying it, however, he detected a sense of gallantry not unlike that which he modestly attributed himself and returned it to Hearne on the condition of its publication. The defeated Governor returned home to discover that he was not the subject of contempt for his losses, but celebrated, the legend of his exploits in exploration having grown in his absence and the geographical significance influencing even the instructions issued to Captain James Cook on his fateful third journey.

Hearne later returned to Hudson Bay to re-establish a trading post at the Churchill River, but declining health forced his retirement to London in 1787, and declining income fuelled his interest in seeing the publication of his *Journey*. Despite the Company's past tendency towards obsessive secrecy, in writing the book's introduction Hearne was granted admission to its archives, where finally he learned details of the voyages of Knight and Scroggs, and doubtless also had access to the account of the fate of Knight given to Moses Norton by the two Inuit boys in 1765. Hearne was compiling his introduction at the very time that Alexander Dalrymple, a noted geographer, published a pamphlet disputing the accuracy of Hearne's mapping, and once again raised the possibility of a Northwest Passage.

Captain Charles Duncan soon embarked on his Company-sponsored efforts to demonstrate its zeal for discovery, and head off the threat posed by renewed criticism. Hearne's literary endeavours need to be considered in a similar context. Like Duncan's voyage, Hearne's introduction, and the release of his journal, serve not only as a defence of himself against the criticism he encountered, but as a defence of the Company against 'ill-grounded and unjust aspersions' that it was 'adverse to making discoveries of every kind . . . being content with the profits of their small capital'. He cites 'motives of interest or revenge' in past criticism of the Company by, among others, Arthur Dobbs, Henry Ellis and Joseph Robson. Since both the Company's reluctance to support Knight's voyage and his apparent subsequent abandonment by them were employed by these critics as evidence of the Company's neglect of exploration, it would seem only logical that Hearne also emphasizes the futility of Knight's endeavours. His authority on the matter was strengthened by his rightful claim, underscored in his *Journey*, of putting 'a final end to' the dispute over the existence of a Northwest Passage through Hudson Bay.

The geologist J. B. Tyrrell, who edited a 1911 edition of Hearne's *Journey*, observed that while ordinarily Hearne recorded his observations with accuracy, 'in the warmth of dispute, when endeavouring to overcome the criticisms or objections of others, he was liable to be carried beyond the points of strict accuracy and, in order to strengthen his argument, fill in blanks in his record from his imagination'. Tyrrell points to this particular trait in explaining the invective which passes as Hearne's biographical sketch of Moses Norton. It is thanks to Hearne that Norton's memory endures as, among other things, a selfish debauchee, a notorious smuggler and a polygamist poisoner. Norton's insane jealousy drove him to murder two women 'because he thought them partial to other objects more suitable to their ages', and even interrupted his death throes in December 1773 when an officer took the hand of one of his fancies, roaring out, 'If I live I'll knock out your brains.' According to Hearne, moments after making

155

this 'elegant apostrophe, he expired in the greatest agonies that can possibly be conceived'. Not one to let a modicum of balance stand in the way of a good vilification, Hearne summarizes his sketch of Norton by suggesting he was, simply put, 'known to live in open defiance of every law, human and divine'.

This tendency to fortify an argument with exaggeration certainly appears to manifest itself again when, in his defence of the actions of the Company, Hearne goes so far as to proffer the opinion, all evidence to the contrary, that after Knight's disappearance, 'the Company were much alarmed for their welfare' and had sent orders for Scroggs 'to go in search of them'. As if that were not enough, Hearne added:

> The strong opinion which then prevailed in Europe respecting the probability of a North West passage by the way of Hudson's Bay, made many conjecture that Messrs. Knight and Barlow [sic] had found that passage, and had gone through it into the South Sea, by way of California. Many years elapsed without any other convincing proof occurring to the contrary. . . .

To support this contention, Hearne dismisses Scroggs's discovery of Knight expedition relics, claiming they 'scarcely amounted to the spoils which might have been made from a trifling accident'. In fact, Scroggs's observations are of critical importance, providing proof of the expedition disaster. Not many years elapsed before the Company became convinced the vessels were lost, and the *Albany* and the *Discovery* were written off by the Company in September 1722, 'being Castaway to the Northward In Hudsons Bay'. The question needs to be asked whether such revisionism, obviously designed to inflate the benevolent pretensions of the Company, was extended to Hearne's own experience at Marble Island.

The established tendency to accord Hearne's published narrative the status of historical authority assumes it to be a matter-of-fact recounting of experience, a view that further fails to consider adequately Hearne's own intention, and that of his publisher, to capitalize on the lucrative market for such travels.

Hearne was paid handsomely for his *Journey*, receiving £200, but his earnings came at a cost, namely the Gothicization of his exploits to accommodate, or at least stimulate his memory of, elements of his travels sufficiently disturbing to satisfy one of that day's prevailing tastes in literature. Hearne sold the manuscript shortly before his death in November 1792, in doing so acknowledging that 'anything in reason shall be allowed to the person that prepares the Work for the Press'. The extent to which reason may have been exceeded in the months following Hearne's death and before the posthumous publication of his *Journey* in 1795, is uncertain.

By analysing differences between Hearne's field notes, an early draft of the *Journey* and then its final published form, the literary historian I. S. MacLaren has built a convincing case for the corruption of the narrative in its depiction of the most famous episode in Hearne's book, the Bloody Fall massacre, where Hearne was a helpless witness to the slayings of slumbering Inuit at the hands of his Indian escorts. In the field notes, the attackers had 'killed every soul before they had the power to rise', but by the time Hearne's manuscript reached print, the plot had been altered, the effect of the changes to add dramatic suspense. Among them is the introduction of the horrifying death of a young woman, stuck with a spear, 'twisting around my legs'. After Hearne disentangles himself from her dying grasps, the grisly epidode ends with the woman transfixed to the ground 'like an eel'. Argues MacLaren, 'No one – man or woman, even Gothic heroine – could entwine around the legs of Hearne the bystander unless the Inuit were either defending themselves or fleeing their assailants. If the field note is fact, they did neither.' Without the benefit of field notes describing Hearne's experiences at Marble Island, it is impossible to undertake a similar comparison with regard to the introduction's treatment of the disaster site and the account received from the Inuit informants. Yet the account given of the last survivors of the Knight expedition appears to have been written in the Gothic manner of the book's most famous (or notorious) scene. Following a direction quintessentially Gothic in instilling a sense of foreboding, the passage serves distinctly dramatic purposes in terms of both the narrative's structure and its intrepid first-person narrator.

Fundamentally, the inclusion of the Knight tragedy may reflect a desire to adhere to the prevailing myth of discovery, establishing the pattern of the quest by first underscoring the insurmountable odds to be overcome by Hearne, the intrepid explorer. Despite the nature of Hearne's journey, and his dependence on the Indians, the notion of triumphant discovery still dominates his narrative. This is perhaps most evident when Hearne, at the Coppermine River, erects a memorial to 'take possession of this coast, on behalf of the Hudson's Bay Company', an act notably unrecorded in surviving copies of his field notes. How he intended to enforce this extravagant territorial claim, when forced to rely on his Indian escorts for his bare survival, is less certain.

Taken in such a context it would seem only natural, in order to underscore the magnitude of his considerable geographical accomplishments and to emphasize his role in bringing about a transformation in the manner of exploration, that Hearne would require a point of comparison, in short, a foil. In the introduction to his *Journey*, that distinction fell on Captain James Knight. While in his depiction of the deaths of the last survivors of the Knight expedition, Hearne celebrates the dauntless courage of the individual, even hailing Knight himself

Human remains at Bloody Fall. Detail of 1821 drawing by
Lieutenant George Back, RN.

as a 'bold adventurer', implicit in his telling is an indictment of exploration as practised by Knight:

> Notwithstanding the experience Mr Knight might have had of the Company's business, and his knowledge of those parts of the Bay where he had resided, it cannot be supposed he was well acquainted with the nature of the business in which he then engaged. . . .

Knight based his endeavours on the 'slender and imperfect accounts of Indians,' Hearne writes, 'who at that time were little known, and less understood'.

Notwithstanding his own experience at Marble Island, there is compelling physical evidence at the site to suggest that Hearne's depiction of the disaster is itself a slender and imperfect account. Hearne's observations on Knight's ruined shelter, the condition and location of the vessels, and other relics of the disaster, are themselves largely accurate. The error may then result from his misinterpretation of the artefacts and testimony he had encountered, but enough difficulties arise from his interpretation to raise the question of whether the portrayal was not only wrong, but intentionally so. A few days before his death in November 1792, Hearne was purportedly heard to say 'he could lay his hand on his heart and say he had never wronged any man of sixpence'. It is less certain that he could make the same claim of his treatment of the memory of Captain James Knight.

12

DEAD SILENCE

'Please God to spare my Life & health and if it is to be done
& any Man can do it I shall,' Knight resolved in 1716, 'tho it
has been my Missfortune always to have nothing but fatique
& trouble in this Country.' By any common measure Knight's
misfortune in the end became a dreadful spectacle, the collective loss of forty lives. After such a failure there is an inevitable
analysis of reasons, and conflicting theories expounded, but the
resulting implication remains essentially the same, designed so
as to induce judgement: Knight's vision had been a delusion.
His whole conception of geography was grotesquely flawed, his
estimations of mineral riches crude and illusory. Nearly three
centuries of pathos are invested in that assumption of forlorn
hope, which reaches its wretched fulfilment with the tragedy
of shipwrecked sailors on a grim Arctic island. It would be, by
its very futility, a complete realization of the contrary qualities
of heroism and folly represented by five centuries of Arctic
exploration, except that the door has now been unfastened to
another possibility.

James Knight does not easily fit the categories into which
northern explorers are meant to fall. By both his great age
and responsibilities, and by his temperament, Knight failed
to adhere neatly to the image of adaptation in exploration
symbolized by the famous journey of Samuel Hearne. Yet his
very life's experience also makes him ill-suited for inclusion
among the ranks of those whose tragic failure is attributed to
unpreparedness for the rigours of the climate or an inability to
cast aside cultural stereotypes. Knight had listened to the Slave

Woman, to the aboriginal peoples of the country, and through them encountered a landscape no other European had. More than half a century before Hearne's journey, Knight had laid the foundations for it, and not only by the travels undertaken on his behalf by William Stuart and Richard Norton. Knight moved beyond convention, convinced that he had some special apprehension, and insisted, especially in the last years of his life, on conducting his career and endeavours on the basis of his own themes. It is there, with the character of Knight, that one final consideration rests. What would Knight have done, assuming he survived that first winter? Would he have glared out from his refuge, defeated by his circumstances, in terror of the unknown Inuit, paralysed by the ice; a man of great age, living through long nights for that one day when the cold sun would give him his freedom? The first explorers in the Arctic clung fast to their ships, their means of passage, during hard winters. Never straying, their discoveries were limited to the immediate horizon. That is where the Knight expedition must be judged differently.

Physical evidence fundamentally alters the consideration of the fate of Knight by closing the gap of time to a few months – two, perhaps three, months in the spring of 1720. That is the period for which the light fails. We know what went on before that time, the arrival of the *Albany* and the *Discovery* in the autumn of 1719, the securing of the vessels, and, anticipating the severe climate, the construction of a considerable shelter in the days before the cold deepened. Hunts were carried out. The possibility that the expedition pursued a whale fishery is suggested by whalebone at the site. From the quantity of coal burned, from the layer of detritus and soot within the structure, and the food remains, there is evidence of occupation of the site during the impenetrable depths of winter.

We know also what followed: the dereliction of the house while the ground remained frozen, perhaps in the spring, as late as June, and the abandonment of one or two vessels that according to logbooks kept by nineteenth-century whalers, and earlier observations of ice conditions, would have been freed from the land floe by no later than July. Given repeated examples of vessels entering a winter harbour in Hudson Bay on a high autumn tide, then the crews finding themselves faced with months of continual cutting, digging and blasting to get the ships clear the following year, it is possible that Knight's expedition found itself in a similar trap. Still it is unimaginable that, had there been any survivors at that time, especially those then able to endure a second winter, as Hearne's account indicates five did, they would not have availed themselves of the opportunity to escape Marble Island, even by small boat. Surely, if Jens Munk and two others were capable a century earlier of reaching Denmark after enduring the great horror of their expedition disaster, Knight's weakened sailors, even crippled with scurvy, would have had the strength and seamanship to make it at least as far as the Company's fort at the Churchill River. It is, then, on that little while – from perhaps April, to July 1720 – that three centuries of unknowing is founded.

It is impossible, either from the historical record, or physical evidence, to establish a precise chronology of events for those lost weeks. There lies the darkness of the Knight expedition mystery. It is a confounding problem, and because time has made evidence itself a disappearing resource, the possibility exists that the fate of the Knight expedition may never, finally, be fully understood. The process of scientific analysis, though, has liberated the expedition from the constrictions of historical convention. There is evidence, both historical, and from assessment of the site, not only to confront existing theories, but ultimately to move beyond them. Here, human remains, or the absence of human remains, play an integral part. The debate over Knight's fate has hinged on the contradictory interpretations of Scroggs and Hearne. In fact, precious little endures either in surviving historical accounts, or at the wintering site, in support of either theory for the source of destruction of the entire expedition.

Curiously, considering all the evidence collected, nothing discounts the controversial account provided by Master John Scroggs, making the loss of his journal all the more frustrating. Beyond his own observation of an Inuk male with a cutlass wound on his face, the case for Scroggs rests largely on negative evidence: the absence of a graveyard representing the bulk of the forty expedition members. What else can be said for Scroggs amounts to no more than circumstantial evidence, the presence of some scattered human bone and teeth on the surface inside and in the immediate vicinity of the house, the presence of one expended musket ball found inside the structure and an Inuit leister, which could serve as a formidable weapon in combat. Scroggs's interpretation cannot be ruled out by this, yet it is hardly proof of an Inuit onslaught and Knight's last stand. Each of these clues can just as easily be employed to support the opposing interpretation, that the surface human remains could represent Hearne's last survivors, too ill from sickness and starvation to have conducted a proper burial. The spent musket ball could have been associated with meat gained by hunting, the leister evidence only of close contact, perhaps the purchase of meat by trade, or the later demolition of the house. It is other evidence that undermines Hearne's account, not this. What seems most apparent is that, irrespective of the cause of deaths of those few men, and assuming there are other remains not yet located, there are still a substantial number of expedition members not represented at the site at all. While physical evidence has narrowed the gap of time, it has served only to expand the Knight mystery geographically.

The image of shipwrecked sailors on a remote island is a romantic ideal, and in the context of the Knight expedition, one entirely in keeping with the allegorical traditions of the popular image of the castaway. Like Defoe's Crusoe, Knight's fate can be viewed as punishment for obstinately adhering to foolish inclinations. But while Marble Island is an exotic setting, it is hardly remote from land. The Inuit regularly traversed the channel separating Marble Island from the mainland, at its narrowest representing a crossing of less than 15 kilometres. Nor was this talent limited to those in possession of the indigenous way of life. In the nineteenth century whalers too crossed back and forth to the mainland in spring, usually by boat, but sometimes on foot after the formation of an ice bridge between the rims of thick coastal ice which form months earlier.

The ice conditions varied dramatically according to weather conditions and the tide, although the chill of the Little Ice Age during Knight's time would have favoured formation of a continuous ice bridge. The Bay is wrongly seen as a formidable barrier.

The crossing was not always without incident. In April 1866 six men from the British whaler *Ocean Nymph* reached the mainland by boat to trade, but the conditions forced their return by foot over the drift ice, in the process of which two took a temporary plunge into freezing water. A similar incident occurred in January 1878 when the surveyor Heinrich Klutschak and W.H. Gilder, members of lieutenant Frederick Schwatka's sledge search for records or relics of the Franklin expedition, accompanied nearly sixty Inuit to the island. Near the midway point Gilder went through the ice. After he clambered out, his pants were found to be both frozen stiff and frozen fast, 'greatly impeding' efforts to keep him moving. Such incidents were, however, the exception. In the winter of 1878-9, Arctic harpooners from New Bedford's *Abbie Bradford* described crossing the 'smooth' stretch of ice to hunt, shooting six foxes and eight rabbits, and returning to Marble Island all in one day.

Further witness was given to the ability of Knight expedition crewmen to cross the sea ice when Bill Gawor made the difficult solo journey from Rankin Inlet to Marble Island and back in April 1991, crossing the maze of hummocks with a snowmobile and komatik. The technology provided no advantage as Gawor spent much of the three hours either dragging or pushing the vehicle, which regularly became stuck in the jumble. Matters were made more difficult by a light, fluffy snow cover that served to conceal gaps created by movement of the ice. Gawor, however, was no worse for the journey, one that would assuredly have posed no greater obstacle long ago to members of the Knight expedition.

Driven from their refuge by 'utmost extremity' in an attempt to reach the Churchill River in the spring or summer of 1720, or simply journeying to the mainland when temperatures had moderated but the ships remained ice-bound, either to hunt,

Travelling in Hudson Bay.

trade or to explore the new lands and reveal their treasure, the expedition members had means of escape. Given the significance of the evidence of the expedition's ability to obtain fresh meat, and Knight's history of defiance when confronted with great obstacles, there is compelling reason to believe the search did not end at Marble Island.

Berley and Vaughan were under specific order to 'as Often as Conveniently you can to send your Boats to the Shoar side' in order to measure the tides 'and to make Such Discoveries and Obtain all such Trade as you can'. Even at the Churchill River, when surrounded by such an 'abundance of Iskemays Tents that it looked like a Town', and confronted with his own fear of violence, Knight sent his men on hunts, and in parties to collect wood, ranging considerable distances. Still more telling, he sent a boy, Richard Norton, out into the Barren Lands in search of the Northern Indians and his great treasure. Knight had even sought to initiate a trade with the Inuit, dangling little gifts about the Churchill River and sending Vaughan northwards along the coast precisely to that end. Knight feared the Inuit, but he did not shrink from contact with them. He was drawn by more urgent concerns, and at Marble Island that urgency would have been still more acutely felt. He must have counted the days, the weeks, as they dwindled past, knowing this was the end of that splendid chance.

Most compelling of all, there are those remote memories, too fantastic to be true – those conveyed to Richard Staunton in April 1721, the spectre that 'our Country men' – Englishmen – had traded with the Copper Indians the previous summer, giving them 'a great Deale of Iron'. The large party of Northern Indians who carried these tidings to Prince of Wales's Fort further promised that the Copper Indians themselves would pay a visit the post in the months to come, to which Staunton added, 'I pray God may prove trouth.' Three months later truth was borne out, a delegation of Copper Indians arrived at the Churchill River to tell of 'great hills of Copper, but it is so farr'. There were even reports of a peace having been forged between the Indians and the Inuit.

Then there is that other haunting suggestion, that of Captain

Francis Smith, who undertook a series of Company sloop voyages to trade with the Inuit at Whale Cove commencing eighteen years after the Knight expedition's disappearance. There, on the mainland coast south-west of Marble Island, Smith was shown a boy the Inuit called 'English Mane, alluding to his being an English Man', a boy apparently of mixed ancestry and of an age seemingly consistent with 'the Time of these Peoples Misfortune'. The conclusion drawn is the stuff of legend, the possibility that 'one or more of the people might get Ashore and live sometime amongst the Eskemaux'.

In the end, had expedition members wandered from their refuge, perhaps drawn by Knight's vision into some deeper unknown, it is inconceivable that Knight would have been among them. Surely of any, he is among the dead of Marble Island, near the cold waters of the same immense bay where two decades earlier his search had begun. Whereas Coronado had retreated from Kansas and the failure of Quivira, for Knight there was no retreat. The very instructions carried by the expedition anticipate 'Capt James Knight being Dead' while on his discovery, finally wasted by the conceit of constant desire. Yet in a very real sense his journey was brought to a fulfilment, one drawn of Knight's own system of perception, where neither victory nor failure finally mattered. It was a question of how one saw distance, magnitude and situation of objects considerably remote.

At Thanadelthur's passing Knight wrote gravely that nothing in his life laid so heavily on him as 'the Loss of her'. He had, through her, glimpsed the distant riches he desired and an unknown world. It was by her apprehension and that of the aboriginal people of a continent that Knight crossed immense distances and remote landscapes. He traversed 'the great Barren Desarts' where there were no trees for fires and barely enough food to keep alive. He had seen the granite shores of Great Slave Lake and the pitch of the Athabasca tar sands. He gazed upon the Canadian Rockies, mountains 'so high that they Reach allmost the sky'. The people encountered seemed as strange as the lands; a faraway mountain tribe that 'garnish themselves with a White Mettle and hangs it in their noses and ears', and, upon the 'West Side of America where the Land is very Mountanious', gold was washed from the ground in great rains, and every summer were seen, at the very edge of vision, the pilots of distant ships sailing on a western sea.

Finally, there was an 'abundance of Copper . . . great hills and Mountains of it and that sometimes they find great Lumps of Copper tumbles out of the Clifts to ye Banks of the River'. It was the Coppermine and September Mountains, and the Coppermine River, emptying into Coronation Gulf and the waters of the Northwest Passage. Nearly three centuries after the disappearance of the Knight expedition, the Coppermine area remains the source of considerable geological interest. In the late 1960s the discovery of high-grade copper deposits in the area resulted in the Coppermine Rush, the largest staking rush in the history of mining in Canada. Seventy mining companies participated, and over forty thousand claims were recorded.

Was it delusion, this particular way of seeing?

APPENDIX 1

SAILING ORDERS and INSTRUCTIONS, 1719

These are the complete texts of the original instructions issued to Captain James Knight, Captain George Berley and Captain David Vaughan, in the Hudson's Bay Company Archives, Provincial Archives of Manitoba (HBCA A. 6/4, fo. 39d, fo. 32d–33, fo. 38, fo. 38d–39).

A Draft of Capt James Knights Instructions, 1719.

Upon the Expeerience wee have had of y^r Ability and Conduct in the Managem^t of our Affairs wee have Upon your Aplication to us fitted out the Albany Frigg^{tt} Capt Geo Berley Commander, The Discovery Capt David Vaughan Commander, Upon a Discovery to the Northward & to y^t End have Given you Power and Authority to act and do all things Relating to the Said Voyage (the Navigation of the Said Shipp and Sloop Only Excepted) and have Given our Said two Command^{rs} Orders & Instructions to that Purpose

You are with the first Opertunity of Wind and Weath^r to Depart Gravesend on your Intended Voyages by Gods Permission to find out the Streight of Annian in Order to Discover Gold and Other Valuable Comodities to the Northward According to the tenor of y^r Articles wth us. Which wee hope you will use y^r Utmost Endeavours to

169

Effect, and do Expect you will Husband Everything to the best Advantage wee Further Order You that in Case you should meet our Gov^{nr} $\wedge$ ^{CAP} Henry Kelsey in your Discovery, or any other Person Deputed from him, or from any of our Command^{rs} or Chiefs of any of our Factories that you show them all Possible Respect, and Neither Molest or hinder them, nor Suffer them to be Molested or hindered in their Business or Affairs, by any Person or Persons on Board Either of ye Shipps Under y^r Command, So Wishing you a Prosperous Voyage and safe return to us, wee Remain

Gravesend The
4 June 1719

Y^r Loving Friends

The Underwritten is to be Sealed up and not to be opened but in Case of the Death of Capt James Knight, 1719

Capt James Knight being Dead wee do hereby Order & Direct that the Persons hereafter named or the Major Part of them have the sole Direction of all Affairs Relating to our Shipp Albany Friggt and Discovery Sloop and the Effects on Board them, for our use Viz: Capt Geo Berley ///////////////////
Capt Berley's 2d mate Capt Vaughans Chief Mate
Capt David Vaughan and $\wedge$ Mr Alez Apthorpe first of all we Order you to Proceed on your Intended voyage to the Latitude 64 Degrees & Endeavour to find out ye Streights of Anian, and to make what Discoveries you Posibly can, and to obtain all sorts of Trade & Commerce for such Comodities as shall be for the Companies Advantage Espécally to find out the Gold and Copper Mines if possible According to the Directions which Capt James Knight will have Left behind him for that Purpose in Writing, and after You have Obtain the Best Cargoe you Can, then make the best of your way Directly home for the Port of London, without Touch^g at any port or Place; But in Case of your Utmost Extremity and not to Break Bulk

Wee do likewise Order you to keep and Bring home with you The Original Book of Minuits and Orders of your Journals, and Transactions in Your Councils, Signed by those Presants at Every meeting Which you are to Deliver us upon y^r Arrival

Wee also Order you do not touch at any of our Factories nor come into any port or trade at any Place to the Southwd of 64 Degrees, north Latitude nor Come to Churchill River Port Nelson River or Hayes River, but in Case of the Utmost Extremity Only to Preserve Shipps Sloop & Mens Lives, and During ye Stay Under such Extremity, to be Absolutely Under the Direction and Governm^t of our Govr or Chief at such Port factory or Setlement Where you shall be, and to be Suplyd with what necessaries you Shall be in want of, Giving Receipts for what shall be Deliverd You

And in Case you should meet with our Govr Capt Hen Kelsey in Your Discovery or any Person or Persons Deputed from him or from any of our Comand^{rs} or Chief from any of our Factories or Setlem^{ts}, that you show them all Posible Respect, and Neither Molest Hinder them, Nor Suffer them to be Molested or hindered in their Business or Affairs, by any Person or Persons, belonging to Either of y^e Shipps under your Command, so wishing you all possible Success wee Remain.

Y^r Loving Friends

Sailing Orders and Instructions to Capt Geo: Berley, 1719

In the first Place wee Require you to have Prayers day =ly Read on Board your Shipp According to the Service of the Church of England.

2dly You are also with the first Opertunity of Wind and Weather to Sail our Shipp Albany Frigg^{tt} Under your Comand to what Place Capt James Knight shall Order you to Sail to That is to y^e Northward and Westward of 64 Degrees in

Hudsons Bay and to use your Utmost Endeavour to keep Comp^a with the Discovery Capt David Vaughan Commander, But in Case you should be Separated from the Discovery by Stress of Weather or otherwise in your outward Bound Voyage before you Enter the Streights, then you are to make towards the Island Resolution, and Ply of Thereabouts ten Days, Unless you meet with her sooner, that you may Proceed on your Voyage Together and in all things during the Whole Term of this your Intended Voyage (except the Naviga=ting Part) You are to Obey and Follow the Direction and Orders of Capt James Knight

3dly You have a Quantity of all sorts of Provisions and Other Necessaries on Board, Lett the Same be Expended as Govr Knight shall from time to time Direct and Order, and that all Y^r Officers on Board, as Boatswain, Gunner, Stewerd, Carpenter & Cook Deliver to you a Weekly Account of all Expences both of Provisions Stores & Other Necessaries, Which is to be wrote out Fair and Produced to the Committee upon your arrival, before the said officers shall Recieve their Respective Wages

Lastly. you are also upon Y^r arrival with us to Deliver in your Journal and your 2^d Mates, With all Other Journals kept on Board your Shipp if you Can Discover Any, and wish you a prosperous voyage we remain

ye Loveing Friends

Sailing Orders and Instructions to Capt David Vaughan, 1719

In the First Place wee Require you to have Prayer Dayly Read on Board your Sloop According to the Service of the Church of England

2^{ly} You are also with the First Opertunity of Wind and Weather to Sail our Sloop Discovery Under your Command to what Place Capt James Knight shall Order you to Sail to, that is to the Northw^d and Westw^d of 64 Degrees in Hudsons

Bay and to use your Utmost Endeavour to keep Comp^a with the Albany Frigg^{tt} Capt Geo Berley Commander, But in Case you Should be seperated from the Albany by Stress of Weather or Otherwise in your outward bound Voyage, before you Enter y^e Streights, then you are to make towards the Island Resolution and Ply of There=abouts for Ten Days Unless you meet with her Sooner, that you may Proceed on your Voyage Together and in all things During the Whole Term of This your Intended Voyage (Except y^e Navigating part) you are to Obey and follow the Direction and Orders of Capt James Knight

3dly [But in Case you have Stayed Ten Days at the Island Resolution and do not meet with the Albany in that time you are then to proceed to the Latitude 64 Degrees North Latitude and from thence Northward to Endeavour to find out the Streights of Anian, and as Often as Conveniently you can to send your Boats to the Shoar side in order to find how high the Tide Rises and W^{ch} Point of the Compas the flood Comes from, and to make Such Discoveries and Obtain all such Trade as you Can,] but to take Especiall care to Return Back before you are in Danger of being frozen up, and make the best of your way homeward so as to be with us the Next Fall.

4^{thly} You having a Quantity of all Sorts of Provisions and Other Necessaries on Board, Lett them be Expended as Govr Knight shall from time to time Direct and Order, and that all your officers on Board, as Boatswain, Gunner, Steward Carpenter & Cook Deliver you a Weekly Acc^{tt} of All Expences both of Provisions and other Stores and Necesaries which is to be wrote out fair and Producd to the Committee Upon y^r Arrival, before the Said Officers Shall Receive their Respective Wages

Postscript

You are also upon your Arrival wth us to Deliver in your Journal Together with your Mates and all Other Journals kept on Board y^r Sloop if you Can Discover Any so wishing you a prosperous voyage wee Remain

Gravesend
June ye 4th 1719

Y^r Loving Friends

APPENDIX 2

Excerpt from the Introduction to A JOURNEY From Prince of Wales's Fort in Hudson's Bay, To THE NORTHERN OCEAN, By Samuel Hearne

This is the complete text of Samuel Hearne's account of the Knight expedition from the Introduction to *A Journey From Prince of Wales's Fort In Hudson's Bay, To The Northern Ocean. Undertaken by order of the Hudson's Bay Company, for the Discovery of Copper Mines, a North West Passage, &c. In the Years 1769, 1770, 1771 & 1772.* London: A. Strahan and T. Cadell. 1795. Bruce Peel Special Collections Library, University of Alberta.

The natives who range over, rather than inhabit, the large track of land which lies to the North of Churchill River, having repeatedly brought famples of copper to the Company's Factory, many of our people conjectured that it was found not far from our fettlements; and as the Indians informed them that the mines were not very diftant from a large river, it was generally fuppofed that this river muft empty itfelf into Hudfon's Bay; as they could by no means think that any fet of people, however wandering their manner of life might be, could ever traverfe fo large a track of country as to pafs the

Northern boundary of that Bay, and particularly without the affiftance of water-carriage. The following Journal, however, will fhew how much thofe people have been miftaken, and prove alfo the improbability of putting their favourite fcheme of mining into practice.

The accounts of this grand River, which fome have turned into a Strait, together with the famples of copper, were brought to the Company's Factory at Churchill River immediately after its firft eftablifhment, in the year one thoufand feven hundred and fifteen; and it does not appear that any attempts were made to difcover either the river or mines till the year one thoufand feven hundred and nineteen, when the Company fitted out a fhip, called the Albany Frigate, Captain George Barlow*, and a floop, called the Difcovery, Captain David Vaughan. The fole command of this expedition, however was given to Mr. James Knight, a man of great experience in the Company's fervice, who had been many years Governor at the different Factories in the Bay, and who had made the firft fettlement at Churchill River. Notwithftanding the experience Mr. Knight might have had of the Company's bufinefs, and his knowledge of thofe parts of the Bay where he had refided, it cannot be fuppofed he was well acquainted with the nature of the bufinefs in which he then engaged, having nothing to direct him but the flender and imperfect accounts which he had received from the Indians, who at that time were little known, and lefs underftood.

Thofe difadvantages, added to his advanced age, he being then near eighty, by no means difcouraged this bold adventurer; whoe was fo prepoffeffed of his fuccefs, and of the great advantage that would arife from his difcoveries, that he procured, and took with him, fome large iron-bound chefts, to hold gold duft and other valuables, which he fondly flattered himfelf were to be found in thofe parts.

The firft paragraph of the Company's Orders to Mr. Knight on this occafion appears to be as follows:

"To Captain James Knight.

"SIR,   4th June, 1719.
"From the experience we have had of your abilities in the management of our affairs, we have, upon your application to us, fitted out the Albany frigate, Captain George Barlow, and the Difcovery, Captain David Vaughan Commander, upon a difcovery to the Northward; and to that end have given you power and authority to act and do all things relating to the faid voyage, the navigation of the faid fhip and floop only excepted; and have given orders and inftructions to our faid Commanders for that purpofe.

"You are, with the firft opportunity of wind and weather, to depart from Gravefend on your intended voyage, and

---

* Captain Barlow was Governor at Albany Fort when the French went over land from Canada to befiege it in 1704. The Canadians and their Indian guides lurked in the neighbourhood of Albany for feveral days before they made the attack, and killed many of the cattle that were grazing in the marfhes. A faithful Home-Indian, who was on a hunting excurfion, difcovering thofe ftrangers, and fuppofing them to be enemies, immediately returned to the Fort, and informed the Governor of the circumftance, who gave little credit to it. However, every meafure was taken for the defence of the Fort, and orders were given to the Mafter of a floop that lay at fome diftance, to come to the Fort with all proffible expedition on hearing a gun fired.

Accordingly, in the middle of the night, or rather in the morning, the French came before the Fort, marched up to the gate, and demanded entrance. Mr. Barlow, who was then on the watch, told them, that the Governor was afleep, but he would get the keys immediately. The French hearing this, expected no oppofition, and flocked up to the gate as clofe as they could ftand. Barlow took the advantage of this opportunity, and inftead of opening the gate, only opened two port holes, where two fix-pounders ftood loaded with grape fhot, which were inftantly fired. This difcharge killed great numbers of the French, and among them the Commander, who was an Irifhman.

Such an unexpected reception made the remainder retire with great precipitation; and the Mafter of the floop hearing the guns, made the beft of his way up to the Fort; but fome of the French who lay concealed under the banks of the river killed him, and all the boat's crew.

The French retired from this place with reluctance; for fome of them were heard fhooting in the neighbourhood of the Fort ten days after they were repulfed; and one man in particular walked up and down the platform leading from the gate of the Fort to the Launch for a whole day. Mr. Fullarton, who was then Governor at Albany, fpoke to him in French, and offered him kind quarters if he chofe to accept them; but to thofe propofals he made no reply, and only fhook his head. Mr. Fullarton then told him, that unlefs he would refign himfelf up as a prifoner, he would moft affuredly fhoot him; on which the man advanced nearer the Fort, and Mr. Fullarton fhoot him out of his chamber window. Perhaps the hardfhips this poor man expected to encounter in his return to Canada, made him prefer death; but his refufing to receive quarter from fo humane and generous an enemy as the Englifh, is aftonifhing.

by God's permiffion, to find out the Straits of Anian, in order to difcover gold and other valuable commodities to the Northward, &c. &c."

Mr. Knight foon left Gravefend, and proceeded on his voyage; but the fhip not returning to England that year, as was expected, it was judge that fhe had wintered in Hudfon's Bay; and having on board a good ftock of provifions, a houfe in frame, together with all neceffary mechanics, and a great affortment of trading goods, little or not thoughts were entertained of their not being in fafety: but as neither fhip nor floop returned to England in the following year, (one thoufand feven hundred and twenty), the Company were much alarmed for their welfare; and, by their fhip which went to Churchill in the year one thoufand feven hundred and twenty-one, they fent orders for a floop called the Whale-Bone, John Scroggs Mafter, to go in fearch of them; but the fhip not arriving in Churchill till late in the Summer following (one thoufand feven hundred and twenty-two).

The North Weft coaft of Hudfon's Bay being little known in thofe days, and Mr. Scroggs finding himfelf greatly embarraffed with fhoals and rocks, returned to Prince of Wales's Fort without making any certain difcovery refpecting the above fhip or floop; for all the marks he faw among the Efquimaux at Whale Cove fcarcely amounted to the fpoils which might have been made from a trifling accident, and confequently could not be confidered as figns of a total fhipwreck.

The ftrong opinion which then prevailed in Europe refpecting the probability of a North Weft paffage by the way of Hudfon's Bay, made many conjecture that Meffrs. Knight and Barlow had found that paffage, and had gone through it into the South Sea, by the way of California. Many years elapfed without any other convincing proof occurring to the contrary, except that Middleton, Ellis, Bean, Chriftopher, and Johnfton, had not been able to find any fuch paffage. And notwithftanding a floop was annually fent to the Northward on difcovery, and to trade with the Efquimaux, it was the Summer of one thoufand feven hundred and fixty-feven, before we had profitive proofs that poor Mr. Knight and Captain Barlow had been loft in Hudfon's Bay.

The Company were now carrying on a black whale fifhery, and Marble Ifland was made the place of rendezvous, not only on account of the commodioufnefs of the harbour, but becaufe it had been obferved that the whales were more plentiful about that ifland than on any other part of the coaft. This being the cafe, the boats, when on the look-out for fifh, had frequent occafion to row clofe to the ifland, by which means they difcovered a new harbour near the Eaft end of it, at the head of which they found guns, anchors, cables, bricks, a fmith's anvil, and many other articles, which the hand of time had not defaced, and which being of no ufe to the natives, or too heavy to be removed by them, had not been taken from the place in which they were originally laid. The remains of the houfe, though pulled to pieces by the Efquinmaux for the wood and iron, are yet very plain to be feen, as alfo the hulls, or more properly fpeaking, the bottoms of the fhip and floop, which lie funk in about five fathoms water, toward the head of the harbour. The figure-head of the fhip, and alfo the guns, &c. were fent home to the Company, and are certain proofs that Meffrs. Knight and Barlow had been loft on that inhofpitable ifland, where neither ftick nor ftump was to be feen, and which lies near fixteen miles from the main land. Indeed the main is little better, being a jumble of barren hills and rocks, deftitute of every kind of herbage except mofs and grafs; and at that part, the woods are feveral hundreds of miles from the fea-fide.

In the Summer of one thoufand feven hundred and fixty-nine, while we were profecuting the fifhery, we faw feveral Efquimaux at this new harbour; and perceiving that one or two of them were greatly advanced in years, our curiofity was excited to afk them fome queftions concerning the above fhip and floop, which we were the better enabled to do by the affiftance of an Efquimaux, who was then in the Company's fervice as a linguift, and annually failed in one of their veffels in that character. The account which we received from them was full, clear, and unreferved, and the fum of it was to the following purport:

When the veffels arrived at this place (Marble Ifland) it was very late in the Fall, and in getting them into the harbour, the largeft received much damage; but on being fairly in, the Englifh began to build the houfe, their number at that time feeming to be about fifty. As foon as the ice permitted, in the following Summer, (one thoufand feven hundred and twenty,) the Efquimaux paid them another vifit, by which time the number of the Englifh was greatly reduced, and thofe that were living feemed very unhealthy. According to the account given by the Efquimaux they were then very bufily employed, but about what they could not eafily defcribe, probably in lengthening the long-boat; for at a little diftance from the houfe there is now lying a great quantity of oak chips, which have been moft affuredly made by carpenters.

Sicknefs and famine occafioned fuch havock among the Englifh, that by the fetting in of the fecond Winter their number was reduced to twenty. That Winter (one thoufand feven hundred and twenty) fome of the Efquimaux took up their abode on the oppofite fide of the harbour to that on which the Englifh had built their houfes*, and frequently fupplied them with fuch provifions as they had, which chiefly confifted of whale's blubber and feal's flefh and train oil. When the Spring advanced, the Efquimaux went to the continent, and on their vifiting Marble Ifland again, in the Summer of one thoufand feven hundred and twenty-one

---

* I have feen the remains of thofe houfes feveral times; they are on the Weft fide of the harbour, and in all probability will be difcernible for many years to come.

It is rather furprifing, that neither Middleton, Ellis, Chriftopher, Johnfton, nor Garbet, who have all of them been at Marble Ifland, and fome of them often, ever difcovered this harbour; particularly the laft-mentioned gentleman, who actually failed quite round the ifland in a very fine pleafant day in the Summer of 1766. But this difcovery was reverved for a Mr. Jofeph Stephens! a man of the leaft merit I ever knew, though he then had the command of a veffel called the Succefs, employed in the whale-fifhery; and in the year 1769, had the command of the Charlotte given to him, a fine brig of one hundred tons; when I was his mate.

they only found five of the Englifh alive, and thofe were in fuch diftrefs for provifions that they eagerly eat the feal's flefh and whale's blubber quite raw, as they purchafed it from the natives. This difordered them fo much, that three of them died in a few days, and the other two, though very weak, made a fhift to bury them. Thofe two furvived many days after the reft, and frequently went to the top of an adjacent rock, and earneftly looked to the South and Eaft, as if in expectation of fome veffels coming to their relief. After continuing there a confiderable time together, and nothing appearing in fight, they fat down clofe together, and wept bitterly. At length one of the two died, and the other's ftrength was fo far exhaufted, that he fell down and died alfo, in attempting to dig a grave for his companion. The fculls and other large bones of thofe two men are now lying above-ground clofe to the houfe. The longeft liver was, according to the Efquimaux account, always employed in working of iron into implements for them; probably he was the armourer, or fmith.

APPENDIX 3

CHRONOLOGIES

Chronology of major events in the life of Captain James Knight

c. 1650	James Knight born
1676, August	Hudson's Bay Company supply ship *Shaftesbury* arrives at Charles Fort at the mouth of the Rupert River in James Bay; James Knight, carpenter and shipwright, is on board, at the beginning of his five-year tour of duty in the Bottom of the Bay
1681	Knight returns to London; soon he is named Chief Factor of Albany Fort, located on the west coast of James Bay, and then becomes Deputy Governor at Hudson Bay
1682, May	Knight sails again for Hudson Bay to take up his post
1683	Knight passed over for governorship; instead, the position is given to Henry Sergeant
1685, September	Knight recalled to London to face charges of private trading; faces tribunal in November, and awaits facing his accuser, Henry Sergeant

1687, October	Governor Henry Sergeant, shamed by his surrender of Albany Fort, returns to London; presses his complaints against Knight, who leaves the Company
1692	Plot to recapture Albany Fort developed, with Knight proposed as the commander, being named Governor of the Bottom of the Bay; Knight then known to be a merchant in London, now middle-aged and financially secure; in March, Knight agrees to lead the campaign on his own terms
1692, August	Knight, aboard the frigate *Royal Hudson's Bay*, along with four other heavily armed frigates, returns to Hudson Bay, later wintering at the Eastmain River, where he prepares his plan of attack and embarks on a mineral search
1693, June	Knight's force recaptures Albany Fort; he remains in the Bay for another four years
1697, August	Knight sets sail for England
1698–1700	Knight returns to Hudson Bay for a short term as Governor of the Bottom of the Bay
1703	Knight listed as a London gentleman, and apparently a successful and influential businessman
1710, February	Knight selected to travel to Holland, along with Sir Bibye Lake, for meetings with the Duke of Marlborough and Viscount Townshend, and to assist in the negotiations over restitution and recovery of posts and land in the Bay then in French hands; negotiations last four months

1710–1714	Knight in London, and suffers with a number of unspecified medical problems
1714, April	Knight, now in his mid-sixties, accepts the commission of Governor to take repossession of York Fort; accompanied by Deputy Henry Kelsey, he returns to the Bay in the *Union*
1714, September	Knight takes possession of York Fort
1714 (late)	Knight meets Thanadelthur, and hears her talk of a distant land full of minerals, animal skins and a strait that could only be a Northwest Passage
1715, May	Hayes River break-up causes flooding and Knight and his men flee the fort
1715, June	Knight sends William Stuart, Thanadelthur, and other volunteers out into the Barrens to try to arrange peace among the warring tribes
1715, summer	Supply ship *Hudson's Bay III*, captained by Joseph Davis, fails to find the entrance to the Hayes River, and returns to England without unloading any of its supplies or cargo, putting the Indian peoples, reliant on the fort supplies and trade, in great peril from starvation over the coming winter
1716, May	The results of Stuart's journey confirms Knight's opinion that there is a Northwest Passage, and a wealth of precious metals, to the north-west
1716, June	Knight is horrified by the condition and suffering of the large numbers of starving Indians now congregated around the

	fort, and worries about the safety of the garrison
1716, August	Situation desperate at York Fort; work on palisades progresses; on 23 August Knight pulls off a bluff, announcing that the supply ship from England will arrive within ten days; within seven days the palisades are complete
1716, 2 September	Guns from supply ship heard, and ship arrives the next day
1716, 8 December	Knight reports in his journal that Thanadelthur has fallen ill
1717, 5 February	Death of Thanadelthur
1717, July	Knight heads north-west to the estuary of the Churchill River after sending an advance party to re-establish a post; he is mortified by the appearance of Inuit in the area; on 18 July Knight sends Richard Norton and two others to find the Northern Indians and give word of the new fort; Norton returns in time for Christmas
1718, September	Henry Kelsey, at York Fort, succeeds Knight as Governor-in-Chief
1718, November	After a difficult passage home which he barely survives, Knight arrives aboard the *Albany* in the Thames; news of his illness is reported
1719, March	The Company Committee discusses a letter from Knight outlining an expedition of discovery; Knight himself soon appears before the Committee; on 24 April the Committee assembles to discuss Knight's proposal, and

they agree to collaborate with him in
a search for gold and copper; on 22
May instructions are drawn up for the
expedition

1719, 5 June   Knight and the rest of his discovery
expedition depart Gravesend in the
frigate *Albany* and sloop *Discovery*

1720?   Death of Captain James Knight

1724, September   Knight's will is executed

Chronology of major events in the discovery of relics and
intelligence relating to the fate of the Knight expedition

1720, July–August   John Hancock, in the *Prosperous*, sent
north from York Fort in pursuit of trade;
hears of Knight expedition's whereabouts
from Inuit

1721, April   Factor Richard Staunton hears from
Northern Indians that the more distant
Copper Indians had encountered white
men the previous summer

1721   Henry Kelsey, during a sloop journey
north from the Churchill River, discovers
items from the lost expedition in the
possession of Inuit – the first evidence of
a disaster; on 9 August Kelsey decides to
return to Churchill rather than conduct a
search for the Knight expedition; arrives
in Churchill on 16 August

1722, July   Master John Scroggs in the sloop
Whalebone sent north from the Churchill
River to look for copper mines;
apparently no attempt was to be made
to look for the lost expedition; finds

evidence of the disaster by chance at Marble Island; on 25 July Factor Richard Staunton records that Scroggs affirms that all of the men of Knight's expedition were killed by Inuit

c. 1738   On one of Captain Francis Smith's northern voyages in the Bay he is shown an Inuk named 'English Mane', a young man with apparent mixed ancestry

1742, August   Captain Christopher Middleton, William Moor and two ships embark on the first attempt by the Royal Navy to find a Northwest Passage; the expedition stopped at Brooke Cobham, which was renamed Marble Island; a great deal of wreckage of the *Albany* and *Discovery* observed

1746, August   Crewmen from two ships (*Dobbs Galley* and *California*, captained by William Moor and Francis Smith, respectively) anchored off Marble Island find fragments from Knight's ships

1765, November   Moses Norton hears stories of the Knight expedition from two Inuit boys from the north-west coast of Hudson Bay; they describe two vessels being lost at Marble Island in the autumn, but the crews were safe and built 'huts' on the near shore; the crews evidently traded iron for food with the local Inuit, but their numbers dwindled, and none survived the winter

1767, July–August   On 22 July Master Joseph Stevens discovers wintering harbour of Knight expedition at the east end of Marble

Island; investigates artefacts and house left by the lost expedition; on 4 August they dig inside house, finding, among other things, a human skull; Hearne goes to site to collect coal; it is recounted in Joseph Stevens's and Magnus Johnston's journals that he (Hearne) found a number of graves

1768, August   After returning to Marble Island, Stevens, with the *Success* and the shallop *Speedwell* commanded by Hearne, discovers a ship's figurehead at the east-end harbour

1769, July–August   Stevens again returns to Marble Island as master of the brig *Charlotte* (Hearne as mate), rendezvousing with Johnston in the *Churchill*; they now know that the discovered relics belong to the Knight expedition; years later Hearne recounts interrogating local Inuit on the disaster; Hearne describes seeing the skeletal remains of the last two Knight expedition members lying above ground near the house; he describes seeing the hulls of both of Knight's vessels in five fathoms of water at the east-end harbour near the house

1791, August   Royal Navy Captain Charles Duncan, in command of a Northwest Passage search in the brig *Beaver*, is the next European after Hearne (1769) to visit the east-end harbour; Duncan and his mate discover parts of a ship, pieces of two anchors, bricks and human bones

1867   American whalers from the *Orray Taft*, anchored in the west-end harbour, collect

coal from the Knight expedition site;
British whalers from the *Ocean Nymph*,
also anchored in the west-end harbour,
visit site to collect coal

NOTES

Many of the sources consulted for facts and quotations are identified or are evident in the text. The following notes are designed to expand on that information. A source is identified on the page of first reference. With regard to current research and publications, various sources may be cited. In certain instances additional information on a subject mentioned in the text is also provided. A complete listing of sources follows. Information regarding any errors or omissions would be gratefully received. Hudson's Bay Company Archives, Provincial Archives of Manitoba appears as HBCA, Public Record Office (UK) as PRO.

1 The Unhappy Sufferers

p. 1 Johnston Journal, 1766. HBCA B 42/a/66. For a full account of the discoveries at Marble Island see Stevens Journal, 1767. HBCA B 42/a/69.

p. 2 Johnston Journal, 1767. HBCA B 42/a/68. Samuel Hearne, Introduction: *A Journey . . . p. xxxi*.

p. 3 Prince of Wales's Fort Journal, 22 Aug 1767. HBCA B 42/a/67.

2 A Point of Darkness

p. 6 Prince of Wales's Fort Journal, 29 Nov. 1765. HBCA B 42/a/64; *The Weekly Journal or Saturday's Post*, 6 June 1719. British Library Burney 194b. There are differing accounts of the origin of the legend that requires visitors to crawl up the beach of Marble Island. One tells of an old woman who wished an island of ice would turn to marble; when it did, her spirit lived there, and people crawled in respect. Told in Kappi, 'Marble Island', p. 13. An account of the Island's sudden appearance from ice and a reference to it being 'regarded with superstition' is given in Hanbury, *Sport and Travel in the Northland of Canada*, p. 53. As early as 1765, Inuit accounts suggest the Inuit shunned the island they called Dead Man's Island, Prince of Wales's Fort Journal, 29 Nov. 1765. HBCA B 42/a/64.

p. 7 For a summary of the early voyages see Wallis, 'England's Search for the Northern Passages in the Sixteenth and Early Seventeenth Centuries', pp. 453–72.

p. 8 Hudson's exploits are recorded in Asher, *Henry Hudson, The Navigator*, and Davis's in Markham, *The Voyages and Works of John Davis, The Navigator*.

p. 10 James's dramatic account of his voyage remains the most stirring of all Arctic narratives and is widely available in reprint. In this case the source was the original 1633 edition, James, *The Strange and Dangerous Voyage of Captaine Thomas James*. London: John Legatt.

p. 11 For Foxe's account see Christy (ed.), *The Voyages of Captain Luke Foxe of Hull and Captain Thomas James of Bristol, In Search of a North-west Passage, In 1631–32*. Beattie's investigation into the fate of the Franklin expedition is described in Beattie & Geiger, *Frozen In Time*.

p. 12 For a reference to Capt. Charles Francis Hall's interest in the Knight expedition see pp. 55–6, Nourse, J. E., *Narrative of the Second Arctic Expedition made by Charles F. Hall*. Washington: Government Printing Office. 1879. Beattie's original research design for investigating the Knight expedition disaster is found in Reed, David W. (ed.). 1990. *Spirit of Enterprise: The 1990 Rolex Awards*. Bern: Buri.

3 The Last Place in North America

p. 16 For further biographical information on Knight see Kenney, *The Founding of Churchill*, pp. 3–108, and Davies (ed.), *Letters from Hudson Bay 1703–40*, pp. 394–410. Knight's career in the context of the great picture of the Hudson's Bay Company's history is found in various references within Rich, *Hudson's Bay Company 1670–1870*, Vol. One 1670–1763. For a definitive account of events leading up to the Knight expedition and its preparations see Williams, 'James Knight and the Strait of Anian' in *The British Search for the Northwest Passage in the Eighteenth Century*, pp. 1–30.

p. 25 London Minute Book, 14 March 1692 HBCA A 1/14; London Minute Book, 18 April 1692 HBCA A 1/14.

p. 26 French version of events at Albany appears in Tyrrell (ed.), *Documents Relating to the Early History of Hudson Bay*. Information on Knight's prisoner is in London Minute Book, 29 Nov. 1693 HBCA A 1/16.

p. 32 For Knight's list of eight conditions for assuming the governorship see London Minute Book, 20 May 1713. HBCA A 1/33. Kelsey's career is summarized in Davies (ed.), *Letters From Hudson Bay 1703–40*, pp. 376–94. See also Doughty & Martin, Introduction, in *The Kelsey Papers*; also Kenney 'The Career of Henry Kelsey'; Kelsey's quaint account in verse of his 1690 journey features the use of metre and rhyme:

> And for my masters I speaking for ym all
> This neck of land I deerings point did call
> Distance from hence by Judgement at ye lest
> From ye house six hundred miles southwest
> Through rivers wch run strong with falls
> thirty three Carriages five lakes in all . . .

p. 34 Knight's York Fort Journal, and that kept during his tenure at the Churchill River, are as follows, York Fort Journal, 1714–15. HBCA B 239/a/1; York Fort Journal, 1715–16. HBCA B 239/a/2; York Fort Journal, 1716–17. HBCA B 239/a/3; Churchill Journal, 1717–18. HBCA B 239/a/3.

4 The Slave Woman

p. 36 Coronado's exploits are described in DeVoto, 'The Children of the Sun', in *The Course of Empire*.

p. 37 Curtis, *The North American Indian*, Vol. 18; Van Kirk,

'Thanadelthur', pp. 40–5. For further reading on the 'Slave Woman' see also Pincott, 'What Churchill Owes to a Woman' pp. 100–103 and Davies (ed.), *Letters from Hudson Bay 1703–40*, pp. 410–13.

p. 39 Ball, 'Synoptic Analysis of Climate for Southwestern Hudson Bay; AD 1720–29' unpublished; also Ball, 'Historical and instrumental evidence of climate: western Hudson Bay, Canada 1714–1850'. Professor of Geography and climatologist Ball has published extensively on the climate of the eighteenth and nineteenth centuries and its relation to the fur trade. See source list for additional references.

p. 40 The 1742 treatise 'Extraordinary Degrees and Surprizing Effects of cold in Hudson's-Bay North America' is based on observations at Churchill, and is found in Middleton, *A Vindication . . .*, pp. 193–206. A copy of Knight's Orders for the Men's Behaviour is contained in his York Fort Journal, 1714–15. HBCA B 239/a/1.

p. 42 Alexander Apthorp to Committee, 2 Sept. 1716, Davies (ed.), *Letters From Hudson Bay, 1703–40*, pp. 51–3. Knight's instructions to William Stuart, 'Orders w[ch] you are to Observe & Follow as Nere as Possible', dated 27 June 1715, are recorded in his York Fort Journal, ibid. The eighth requires Stuart to 'tell the Indian Woman to Acquaint her Country people & they likewise to Acquaint all their friends Y[t] if at Anytime they see a Vessell wth Sails & Masts or here any great Guns at any time that they should not be afraid but make a smoak for a signall for us to come to them for it is ye English comeing to trade'.

p. 43 Guinard, 'Witiko Among the Tete-De-Boule', *Primitive Man*, pp. 69–71. For a more recent examination of the Windigo (sometimes spelled Witiko), see also Preston, Richard J. 'The Witiko: Algonkian Knowledge and White Man Knowledge', in *Myth*, pp. 111–27. The full account of the 1779 visitation by a Windigo among the Cree at Yort Fort is contained in Umfreville, *The Present State of Hudson Bay*, pp. 40–43. Umfreville explains the Indians complained of being plagued by an evil Being, Whit-ti-co, 'generally described in the most hideous forms'. In the case of the 1779 occurrence he writes, 'The Devil, with hideous howlings, frequented their tent every night. . . . So overcome were they by their apprehensions, that they kept large fires continually burning all night, and sleeping only in the day-time. One of them declared that he had fired his gun at him, but unluckily missed him. He described him to be of human shape, going about with cloaths, and taking prodigious strides over the snow. . . . It proved afterwards, that the formidable enemy that had caused such a panic among them, was nothing more than a night owl'.

p. 44 For a detailed account of the problems encountered during construction of the new York Fort see Ingram, 'York Factory: A Structural History', pp. 1–15.

p. 46 Thomas McCleish to Committee, 23 Aug. 1723. Davies (ed.), *Letters From Hudson Bay 1703–40*, pp. 92–6.

5   Petty Dancers

p. 49 William Stuart's letter to Knight is dated 16 October 1715, and reads in part, 'I hope you are good health but wee are in a starving condition at this time wee still press on in our journey the [Cree] Captain is willing to go through but afraid that wee shall gett no provissions we have eat nothing this 8 days I do not think as I shall see you any more but I have a good heart we have no Buffolo as yett wee are abt a hundred Miles from Churchill River the most part of the Indians has left us I would have write by those Indians as came away before but they would not stay . . .'. A copy of Stuart's letter is found in the York Fort Journal, 22 April 1716. HBCA b 239/a/2.

p. 50 For more on the course of Stuart's journey see Morton, *A History of the Canadian West. . . .*, p. 133.

p. 51 Jenness, 'Hunting Bands of Eastern and Western Canada' in Owen et al, *The North American Indians*, p. 203. Carruthers's testimony appears in Reports from Committees of the House of Commons, Vol. II (1803), pp. 230–1.

p. 52 A discussion of the map attributed to Knight is found in Warkentin & Ruggles, *Manitoba Historical Atlas* p. 86; also Ruggles, *A Country so Interesting*, pp. 30–1. Helm, 'Matonabbee's Map', pp. 20–30; Kindle, 'Classification and Description of Copper Deposits, Coppermine River Area. . .', p. 21; Frankin et al, 'An Examination of Prehistoric Copper Technology and Copper Sources in Western Arctic and Subarctic North America', pp. 4–5.

p. 53 For more on Knight's account of the Athabasca Tar Sands, and Kelsey's later description see Davies (ed.), *Letters From Hudson Bay 1703–40*, p. 404.

p. 57 For a fine description of the phenomenon of Knight's petty dancers, the aurora borealis (Northern Lights), see Lopez, *Arctic Dreams*, pp. 232–6.

p. 61 Study on biting flies is Hocking, B. 1952. 'Protection from northern biting flies'. *Mosquito News*. 12. pp. 91–102. Summarized in Oliver, 'Insects' pp. 422–4, the article includes the conservative estimate of five million mosquitoes per acre found in the area of Hudson Bay. An early encounter, by Frobisher, with biting flies that 'stingeth and offendeth sorelye' is found in Collinson, *The Three Voyages of Martin Frobisher*, p. 286.

p. 63 Munk's account is found in Gosch (ed.), *Danish Arctic Expeditions 1605 to 1620*, Book II, pp. 37–48.

6 Strange Magic

p. 65 Kenney, *The Founding of Churchill*, p. 78.

p. 66 *The Weekly Journal or Saturday's Post*, 22 Nov. 1718. British Library, Burney, 186b. *The Weekly Journal or Saturday's Post*, 20 Dec. 1718. British Library, Burney 186b.

p. 67 Reference to Middleton's early career is found in Middleton, *A Vindication of the Conduct. . .* , p. 41; Middleton's testimony on Knight is found in Dobbs, *Remarks upon Capt. Middleton's Defence*, p. 9. For mortality information see McNamara, 'Mortality trends: historical trends', *International Encyclopedia of Population, Vol. II*, pp. 459–61.

p. 68 Account of Berley's early career is from Hearne, *A Journey. . .*, p. xxiv *n*.

p. 69 Knight on Vaughan from Davies (ed.), *Letters from Hudson Bay*, p. 69. Vaughan's career see ibid, p. 63n. Apthorp's selection for Knight expedition, see HBCA A 6/4, of. 32d. Crew names, HBCA A 1/117 fo. 20d; HBCA A 15/6, 4 June 1719.

p. 70 The report of Knight's strongboxes is not as firm as the Hudson's Bay Company records, and comes from Robson, *An Account of Six Years Residence in Hudson's Bay. . .* , p. 37.

p. 72 Committee to Kelsey, 1719. HBCA A 6/4.

p. 73 *The Weekly Journal or Saturday's Post*, 6 June 1719. British Library, Burney 194b.

7 Dead Man's Island

p. 76 Prince of Wales's Fort Journal, 16 April 1721. HBCA B 42/a/1; Doughty & Martin (eds.), *The Kelsey Papers*, p. 116.

p. 77   For Orders to Captain John Scroggs see 31 June 1722. HBCA B 239/b/3, fo. 11. For summary of Scroggs's abilities and discovery of Knight foremast see Drage *An Account of A Voyage . . .*, pp. 174–7. Staunton writes in Prince of Wales's Fort Journal, 25 July 1722. HBCA B 42/a/2; ibid, 26 July 1722. Two notable surviving accounts of Scroggs's voyage, based on his lost journal, are found in Dobbs, *Remarks*, pp. 113–17, and Drage, *An Account of a Voyage . . .*, pp. 97–8, 174–80. See also Anon., *A Description of the Coast, Tide & Currents in Button's Bay*, p. 11.

p. 78 Estimate of cost of Knight expedition is found in Dobbs, *Remarks*, p. 7.

p. 79 Knight's will reads in part, 'I James Knight of Bisham als Bulsham in the County of Berks Gent being in good health of Body . . . And being now bound out on a voyage to Sea am therefore willing and desirous to settle and dispose of what Temporall Estate it shall please Almighty God to blesse me with as followeth . . . I give and bequeath unto my sone Gilpin Knight one shilling and no more he having been already advanced by me in the world Considerably more than my Circumstances could allow off. All the Rest Residue and Remainder of my Estate both Recall and personall whatsoever . . . I Give Devise and bequeath unto my Loving Wife Elizabeth Knight and her Assigns for ever . . .' The will is dated 3 June 1714. The text of the will is contained in Kenney, *The Founding of Churchill*, pp. 88–9. The original is in the PRO (UK).

p. 81 Dobbs, *Remarks . . .*, p. 5.

p. 82 Moor, *Discovery* Journal, PRO Adm 51/290, Pt. IX; Middleton, *A Rejoinder* . . ., p. 119.

p. 84 Drage, *An Account of a Voyage* . . ., p. 98.

p. 85 For a discussion of Hudson's Bay Company secrecy and Company critics during this period see Williams, 'The Hudson's Bay Company and Its Critics in the Eighteenth Century', pp. 149–71. Testimony from Parliamentary hearings is found in Reports from Committees of the House of Commons, Vol. II (1803). Williams, 'Arthur Dobbs and Joseph Robson: New Light on the Relationship between Two Early Critics of the Hudson's Bay Company', pp. 132–6.

p. 86 Moses Norton records the Inuit boys' account in Prince of Wales's Fort Journal, 29 Nov. 1765, HBCA B 42/a/64.

p. 88 For Walker's entries see Walker Journal, 1759. HBCA B 42/a/35; Walker Journal, 1751. HBCA B 42/a/37; Walker Journal, 1753. HBCA B 42/a/41.

p. 92 For account of 1768 activities at Marble Island see Stevens Journal, 1768. HBCA B 42/a/72; Hearne Journal, 1768. HBCA B 42/1/73; Johnston Journal, 1768. HBCA B 42/a/71.

p. 93 See Johnston Journal, 1769. HBCA B 42/a/75; Stevens Journal, 1769. HBCA B 42/a/76.

8 A Timeless Place

p. 96 Glover, Introduction, in *Letters From Hudson Bay 1703–40*, pp. lvii–lviii; Neatby, 'History of Hudson Bay' in *Science, History and Hudson Bay*, Vol. 1, p. 99.

p. 97 Whymper, *Heroes of the Arctic*, p. 62.

p. 98 Osborn, Lieut. Sherard, *Stray Leaves from an Arctic Journal; or, Eighteen Months in the Polar Regions, in Search of Sir John Franklin's Expedition, in the Years 1850–1*. (London, 1865).

p. 102 Christy. (ed.), *The Voyages of Captain Luke Foxe of Hull and Captain Thomas James of Bristol, In Search of a North-west Passage, In 1631–32*.

p. 103 Drage, *An Account of a Voyage*, p. 95.

p. 106 For geological descriptions of Marble Island see Bell, 'Quartzite from Marble Island', and Tyrrell, 'Description of Marble Island, Hudson Bay'.

p. 108 Parker Journal, 14 June 1867. Kendall Whaling Museum, Sharon, Mass. Reel 31, File 277; Ross, 'Whaling in Hudson Bay, Part II-1866–67' pp. 40–7.

p. 110   Martin, 'Life and Death at Marble Island', pp. 48–56; Tuttle, *Our North Land*, p. 110.

p. 112 Gilder, *Schwatka's Search*, p. 37; Smith and Barr, 'Record of the Sloop *Churchill's* visit to Marble Island in 1787', p. 53.

p. 114 Arima, 'Caribou Eskimo' in *Handbook of North American Indians, Vol. 5, Arctic*, p. 459; Ellis, *A Voyage to Hudson's Bay*, p. 137.

p. 116 Taylor Journal, 28 Aug 1791. HBCA C 1/204, fo. 47. For a reference to Duncan's illness see HBCA C 7/13, fo.1–1d. For an account of Duncan's expedition see Williams, *The British Search for the Northwest Passage in the Eighteenth Century*, pp. 245–8. Duncan to Committee, 8 Sept. 1791. HBCA A 10/1, fo. 30–30d.

p. 117 For a discussion of the treatment of the terrain in terms of the sublime and picturesque see MacLaren, 'Samuel Hearne & The Landscapes of Discovery', pp. 27–40.

p. 118 Frobisher's encounters with the Thule are found in Collinson, *The Three Voyages of Martin Frobisher*; McGhee, 'Thule Culture and the Inuit (A.D. 1000–1600), in *Canadian Arctic Prehistory*, pp. 83–115.

9   The Last Man

p. 121 For accounts of the 1970 and 1971 research see Smith, 'Relics of James Knight', pp. 36–41, Zacharchuk, 'The House That Knight Built', pp. 12–15, Smith & Barr, 'Marble Island; A search for the Knight expedition, August 6–15, 1970; also Smith, 'Marble Island: A Search For The Knight Expedition', unpublished report, Smith, 'Discovery of one of James Knight's ships at Marble Island; a preliminary report', unpublished report.

p. 131 Crew and provisioning lists are found in the Grand Journal HBCA A 15/6; London Rough Minute Book HBCA A 1/117; Grand Leger HBCA A 14/7. For a similar calculation see Williams, *The British Search for the Northwest Passage in the Eighteenth Century*, pp. 10–11.

10 The Phantom Ship

p. 143 For an account of 1971 dives see Smith, 'Discovery of one of James Knight's ships at Marble Island: a preliminary report', pp. 12–14; also, Smith, unpublished report.
p. 147 Hickey, 'An Examination of Processes of Cultural Change among Nineteenth Century Copper Inuit', pp. 13–31.

11 A Gothic Journey

p. 151   Rich (ed.), *James Isham's Observations on Hudsons Bay, 1743*, p. 179.
p. 152 Hearne's accomplishments are summarized in Hume, 'To Walk on the Wind', in *Ghost Camps*, pp. 19–32.
p. 154   Glover, Introduction, in *A Journey From Prince of Wales's Fort . . .*, p. xxxix–xi.
p. 155   Tyrrell, Introduction, in *A Journey From Prince of Wales's Fort . . .*, p. 15.
p. 157   For an analysis of differences between Hearne's field notes and *Journey* see MacLaren, 'Samuel Hearne's Accounts of the Massacre at Bloody Fall, 17 July 1771', pp. 25–51. For a discussion of the reliability of the published accounts as the record of what the traveller actually experienced see MacLaren, 'Exploration/Travel Literature and the Evolution of the Author', pp. 39–68.
p. 158 Greenfield, 'The Idea of Discovery as a Source of Narrative Structure in Samuel Hearne's *Journey To The Northern Ocean*', pp. 189–209.

12 Dead Silence

p. 163 For accounts of crossings between the mainland and Marble Island see Klutschak, *Overland to Starvation Cove*, pp. 34–5, Ferguson, *Arctic Harpooner*, p. 87, Ross, 'Whaling in Hudson Bay' Part II, p. 44.
p. 168 For an assessment of Knight's geographical intelligence see Williams, *The British Search for the Northwest Passage in the Eighteenth Century*, pp. 4–6. Kindle, 'Classification and Description of Copper Deposits, Coppermine River Area . . .', p. 6.

SOURCES

i Newspapers

The Weekly Journal or Saturday's Post, 22 Nov. 1718. British Library, Burney 186b
The Weekly Journal or Saturday's Post, 20 Dec. 1718. British Library, Burney 186b
The Weekly Journal or Saturday's Post, 6 June 1719. British Library, Burney 194b

ii Unpublished

York Fort Journal, 1714–15. HBCA B 239/a/1
York Fort Journal, 1715–16. HBCA B 239/a/2
York Fort Journal, 1716–17. HBCA B 239/a/3
York Fort Journal, 10 Aug. 1720, HBCA B 239/a/5.fo.80d
York Fort Journal, 1721–22. HBCA B 239/a/7
Churchill Journal, 1717–18. HBCA B 239/a/3
Churchill Journal, 1718. HBCA B 42/a/1
Prince of Wales's Fort Journal, 22 Aug. 1767 HBCA B 42/a/67
Prince of Wales's Fort Journal, 29 Nov. 1765 HBCA B 42/a/64
Prince of Wales's Fort Journal, 1720–21. HBCA B 42/a/1
Prince of Wales's Fort Journal, 1721–22. HBCA B 42/a/2

Moor Journal, 1742. PRO Adm 51/290. Pt. IX
Walker Journal, 1750. HBCA B 42/a/35
Walker Journal, 1751. HBCA B 42/a/37
Walker Journal, 1753. HBCA B 42/a/41

Johnston Journal, 1765. HBCA B 42/a/63
Johnston Journal, 1766. HBCA B 42/a/66
Johnston Journal, 1767. HBCA B 42/a/68
Johnston Journal, 1768. HBCA B 42/a/71
Johnston Journal, 1769. HBCA B 42/a/75
Stevens Journal, 1767. HBCA B 42/a/69
Stevens Journal, 1768. HBCA B 42/a/72
Stevens Journal, 1769. HBCA B 42/a/76
Hearne Journal, 1768. HBCA B 42/1/73
Taylor Journal, 1791. HBCA C 1/204. fo. 47
Parker Journal, 1867. Kendall Whaling Museum. Reel 31, File 277

London Minute Book, 1692. HBCA A 1/14
London Minute Book, 1693. HBCA A 1/16
London Minute Book, 1700/01. HBCA A 1/23
London Minute Book, 1701/02. HBCA A 1/25
London Minute Book, 1702/03. HBCA A 1/25
London Minute Book, 1703/04. HBCA A 1/26
London Minute Book, 1704/05. HBCA A 1/27
London Minute Book, 1705/06. HBCA A 1/28
London Minute Book, 1706/07. HBCA A 1/29, fo. 4. fo. 6.
London Minute Book, 1709/10. HBCA A 1/32
London Minute Book, 1711/18. HBCA A 1/33
Apthorp's selection for Knight expedition, see HBCA A 6/4. fo. 32d
Grand Journal HBCA A 15/6
London Rough Minute Book HBCA A 1/117, fos. 13–24d
Grand Leger 1717. HBCA A 14/7

Knight to Staunton, 28 June 1715. HBCA A 6/6
Committee to Knight, 31 May 1717. HBCA A 6/4
Committee to Kelsey, 4 June 1719. HBCA A 6/4
Committee to McCleish, . . . 1719. HBCA A 6/4
Duncan to Committee, 8 Sept. 1791. HBCA A 10/1, fo. 30-30d
On Capt. Charles Duncan HBCA C 7/13, fo. 1-1d
Committee to Kelsey, 26 May 1721. HBCA A. 6/4, fo. 48d-50d
Kelsey to Staunton, 1 Feb. 1719/20. HBCA B 239/b/1, fo. 26-26d

SOURCES

Kelsey to Staunton, 12 April 1720. HBCA B 239/b/1, fo. 26d-27

Orders to Capt. John Scroggs 31 June 1722. HBCA B 239/b/3, fo. 11
HBCA B 59/a/9, fo. 3
HBCA RG 20/6C/8

iii Other

ADAMS, PERCY G. 1962. *Travelers and Travel Liars 1600–1800*.
Berkeley: University of California Press
ANONYMOUS, 1746. *A Description of the Coast, Tides, and
Currents, in Button's Bay*. Dublin
ANONYMOUS, 1749. *Reasons to shew, that there is a great
Probability of a Navigable Passage to the Western American Ocean,
through Hudson's Streights, and Chesterfield Inlet*. London
ANONYMOUS, 1749. Report from the Committee, Appointed
to enquire into the State and Condition of the Countries adjoin-
ing to Hudson's Bay, and of the Trade carried on there. Reports
from Committees of the House of Commons, Vol. II. 1803
ARIMA, EUGENE Y. 1984. 'Caribou Eskimo' In: *Handbook of
North American Indians, Volume 5, Arctic*. Washington: Smith-
sonian Institution
ASHER, G.M. 1869. *Henry Hudson, The Navigator*. London: The
Hakluyt Society
BALL, T.F. 1992. 'Synoptic Analysis of Climate for South-
western Hudson Bay; A.D. 1720–29'. (Unpublished).
BALL, T.F. 1992 'Historical and instrumental evidence of cli-
mate: western Hudson Bay, Canada, 1714–1850' In: *Climate Since
AD 1500*. R.S. Bradley & Philip D. Jones (ed.).
BALL, T.F. 1986. 'Historical evidence and climatic implications
in the boreal tundra transpition in Central Canada'. Climatic
Change 8 (1986) pp. 121–34
BALL, T.F. 1983. 'Migration of geese as an indicator of climate
change in the southern Hudson Bay region between 1715 and
1851'. Climatic Change 5 (1983) pp. 85–93
BARR, WILLIAM (ed.). 1988. *Heinrich Klutschak Overland to
Starvation Cove: With the Inuit in Search of Franklin 1878–1880*.
Toronto: University of Toronto Press

BARROW, JOHN. 1818. *A Chronological History of Voyages into the Arctic Regions; Undertaken Chiefly for the Purpose of Discovering a North-east, North-west, or Polar Passage Between the Atlantic and Pacific: From the Earliest Periods of Scandinavian Navigation, to the Departure of the Recent Expeditions, under the orders of Captains Ross and Buchan.* London: John Murray

BARROW, JOHN (ed.). 1852. *The Geography of Hudson's Bay: Being the Remarks of Captain W. Coats, in many voyages to that locality, between the years 1727 and 1751.* London: The Hakluyt Society

BEATTIE, OWEN and Geiger, John. 1987. *Frozen In Time: The Fate of the Franklin Expedition.* London: Bloomsbury Publishing Ltd

BELL, R. 1884. *Quartzite from Marble Island, Hudson Bay.* Geological Survey of Canada, Report of Progress, 1882–84

BERKELEY, GEORGE. 1910. *A New Theory of Vision.* London: J.M. Dent & Sons

BODDINGTON, A., Garland, A. N., Janaway, R. C. 1987. *Death, Decay and Reconstruction.* Manchester University Press

CHAPPELL, LIEUT. EDWARD. 1817. *Narrative of a Voyage to Hudson's Bay in His Majesty's Ship Rosamond containing some account of the North-eastern Coast of America and of the Tribes Inhabiting That Remote Region.* London: J. Mawman

CHRISTY, MILLER. (ed.). 1894. *The Voyages of Captain Luke Foxe of Hull and Captain Thomas James of Bristol, In Search of a North-west Passage, In 1631–32.* London: Hakluyt Society

[CLUNY, ALEXANDER]. 1769. *The American Traveller: or Observations on the Present State, Culture and Commerce of the British Colonies in America.* London

COLLINSON, RICHARD. 1867. *The Three Voyages of Martin Frobisher In Search of a Passage to Cathaia and India by the North-west.* London: The Hakluyt Society

COOKE, ALAN and Holland, Clive. 1971. 'Chronological List of Expeditions and Historical Events in Northern Canada. III 1713–63'. *Polar Record*, January 1971. 15:97. pp. 503–22

COOKE, ALAN and Holland, Clive. 1978. *The Exploration of Northern Canada, 500 to 1920: A Chronology.* Toronto: The Arctic History Press

SOURCES

CUMMING, W.P., Hillier, S. Quinn, D.B. and Williams, G. 1974. *The Exploration of North America 1630–1776*. New York: G.P. Putnam's Sons

CURTIS, EDWARD S. 1928. *The North American Indian*. Norwood, Massachusetts: The Plimpton Press

DAVIES, K.G. (ed.). 1965. *Letters from Hudson Bay 1703–40*. London: The Hudson's Bay Record Society

DAVIS, JOHN. 1607. *The Seamans Secrets*. London: Thomas Dawson

DAY, ALAN EDWIN. 1986. *Search for the Northwest Passage; An Annotated Bibliography*. New York: Garland Publishing, Inc.

DEFOE, DANIEL. 1965. *Robinson Crusoe*. Edited with an Introduction by Angus Ross. London: Penguin Books

DE VOTO, BERNARD. 1952. *The Course of Empire*. Boston: Houghton Mifflin Company

DOBBS, ARTHUR. 1744. *Remarks upon Capt. Middleton's Defence*. London: Jacob Robinson

DOBBS, ARTHUR. 1744. *An Account of the Countries adjoining to Hudson's Bay, In the North-West Part of America*. London: J. Robinson

DODGE, ERNEST S. 1961. *Northwest by Sea*. New York: Oxford University Press

DOUGHTY, ARTHUR G. and Martin, Chester (eds.). 1929. *The Kelsey Papers*. Ottawa: The Public Archives of Canada and the Public Record Office of Northern Ireland

DOUGLAS, R. and Wallace, J.N. (eds.). 1926. *Twenty Years of York Factory 1694–1714; Jeremie's Account of Hudson Strait and Bay*. Ottawa: Thorburn and Abbott

[DRAGE, THEODORE SWAINE]. 1748–9. *An Account of a Voyage for the Discovery of a North-West Passage by Hudson's Streights, to the Western and Southern Ocean of America*. London

ELLIS, HENRY. 1748. *A Voyage to Hudson's-Bay by the Dobbs Galley and California, In the Years 1746 and 1747, For Discovering a North West Passage*. London: H. Whitridge

FOSS, MICHAEL. 1974. *Undreamed Shores: England's Wasted Empire in America*. London: Harrap

FRANKLIN, U.M., Badone, E., Gotthardt, R. and Yorga,

B. 1981. 'An Examination of Prehistoric Copper Technology and Copper Sources in Western Arctic and Subarctic North America', National Museum of Man Mercury Series, Archeological Survey of Canada, Paper No. 101

FRASER, J. KEITH. 1968. 'Place Names'. From *Science, History and Hudson Bay Volume 1*. C.S. Beals (ed.). Ottawa: Department of Energy, Mines and Resources

GILDER, WILLIAM H. 1881. *Schwatka's Search*. London: Sampson Low, Marston, Searle, and Rivington

GILLESPIE, BERYL C. 1975. 'Territorial Expansion of the Chipewyan in the 18th Century' In: Proceedings, Northern Athapaskan Conference, 1971 Vol. 2, National Museum of Man Mercury Series, Canadian Ethnology Service, Paper No. 27, pp. 351–88

GLOVER, RICHARD. 1958. Editor's Introduction: *A Journey to the Northern Ocean*. Toronto: Macmillan

GOLDSON, WILLIAM. 1793. *An Historical Abridgement of Discoveries in the North of America, collected from Various Authors. With Occasional Notes and Observations*. London

GOSCH, C.C. A. (ed.). 1897. *Danish Arctic Expeditions. Book II*. London: The Hakluyt Society

GOUGH, BARRY M. 1980. *Distant Dominion: Britain and the Northwest Coast of North America*. Vancouver: University of British Columbia Press

GREENFIELD, BRUCE. 1986. 'The Idea of Discovery as a Source of Narrative Structure in Samuel Hearne's Journey to the Northern Ocean'. *Early American Literature*. Volume 21, No. 3 Winter 1986–7

GUINARD, REV. JOSEPH E. 1923?. 'Witiko Among the Tete-de-Boule. *Primitive Man* pp. 69–71

HAKLUYT, RICHARD, 1589. *The Principall Navigations, Voiages and Discoveries of the English nation*. London: George Bishop

HANBURY, DAVID T. 1904. *Sport and Travel in the Northland of Canada*. London: Edward Arnold

HANSEN, THORKILD. 1970. *The Way to Hudson Bay: The Life and Times of Jens Munk*. New York: Harcourt, Brace & World, Inc.

HEARNE, SAMUEL, 1795. *A Journey from Prince of Wales's Fort*

SOURCES

in Hudson's Bay, to the Northern Ocean. Undertaken by order of the Hudson's Bay Company, for the discovery of Copper Mines, a North West Passage, &c. In the Years 1769, 1770, 1771 & 1772. London: A. Strahan and T. Cadell

HELM, JUNE. 1989. 'Matonabbee's Map', *Arctic Anthropology*, Vol. 26 No. 2 (1989) pp. 28–47

HICKEY, CLIFFORD G. 1984. 'An Examination of Processes of Cultural Change among Nineteenth Century Copper Inuit'. *Etudes/Inuit/Studies*, 1984, Vol. 8 No. 1, pp. 13–35

HUME, STEPHEN. 1989. 'To Walk on the Wind' In: *Ghost Camps: Memory and Myth on Canada's Frontier*, pp. 19–32. Edmonton: NuWest Publishers Limited

INGRAM, GEORGE. 1979. 'York Factory: A Structural History', Parks Canada, Manuscript Report Series No. 297

INGRAM, GEORGE. 1979. 'Prince of Wales's Fort: A Structural History', Parks Canada, Manuscript Report Series No. 297

JAMES, THOMAS. 1633. *The Strange and Dangerous Voyage of Captaine Thomas James* London: John Leggatt

JENNESS, DIAMOND. 1955. 'Hunting Bands of Eastern and Western Canada' In: *The North American Indians*. Toronto: Macmillan

JOHNSON, ALICE. 1945. 'First Governor on the Bay.' *The Beaver*, June 1945. pp. 22–5

JOHNSON, ALICE. 1952. 'Ambassadress of Peace.' *The Beaver*, December 1952. pp. 42–5

KAPPI, LEONIE, 1971? 'Marble Island', *North*, Vol. 18. p. 13

KENNEY, JAMES F. 1929. 'The Career of Henry Kelsey.' Transactions of the Royal Society of Canada, 3d. S. v. 23, Sec. II, 1929

KENNEY, JAMES F. (ed.). 1932. *The Founding of Churchill Being the Journal of Captain James Knight, Governor-in-Chief in Hudson Bay, from the 14th of July to the 13th of September, 1717.* Toronto: J.M. Dent and Sons Ltd

KINDLE, E. D. 1972. 'Classification and Description of Copper Deposits, Coppermine River area, District of Mackenzie'. Bulletin 214. Ottawa: Geological Survey of Canada

LAUT, AGNES C. 1908. *The Conquest of the Great Northwest*. New York: The Outing Publishing Company

LAWRENCE, T. E. 1981. *Seven Pillars of Wisdom*. London: Penguin

LEE, SIDNEY (ed.). 1892. 'James Knight'. In: *Dictionary of National Biography Vol. XXXI*. London: Elder & Co.

LOPEZ, BARRY. 1986. *Arctic Dreams: Imagination and Desire in a Northern Landscape*. New York: Charles Scribner's Sons

MacLAREN, I. S. 1984. 'Samuel Hearne's Accounts of the Massacre at Bloody Fall, 17 July 1771'. *Ariel* 22:1, January 1991. pp. 25–51

MacLAREN, I. S. 1992. 'Exploration/Travel Literature and the Evolution of the Author', *International Journal of Canadian Studies*. Spring 1992. pp. 39–68

McGHEE, ROBERT. 1978. Canadian Arctic Prehistory. Ottawa: Government of Canada

MARKHAM, ALBERT HASTINGS (ed.). 1880. *The Voyages and Works of John Davis, The Navigator*. London: The Hakluyt Society

MARTIN, KENNETH R. 1979. 'Life and Death at Marble Island 1864–73'. *The Beaver*, Spring 1979, pp. 48–56

MIDDLETON, CHRISTOPHER. 1743. *A Vindication of the Conduct of Captain Christopher Middleton, in a Late Voyage on Board His Majesty's Ship the Furnace, for Discovering a North-west Passage to the Western American Ocean*. London: Jacob Robinson

MIDDLETON, CHRISTOPHER. 1745. *A Rejoinder to Mr. Dobb's Reply*. London

MORTON, ARTHUR S. 1973. *A History of the Canadian West to 1870–71*. Second edn. Toronto: University of Toronto Press

NEATBY, L.H. 1968. 'History of Hudson Bay.' From: *Science, History and Hudson Bay, Volume 1*. C.S. Beals (ed.). Ottawa: Department of Energy, Mines and Resources

NEWMAN, PETER C. 1985. *Company of Adventurers*. Toronto: Penguin Books

NUTE, GRACE LEE. 1983. *Caesars of the Wilderness*. Second edn. St Paul: Minnesota Historical Society Press

OLIVER, D.R. 1968. 'Insects' From: *Science, History and Hudson Bay, Volume 1*. C.S. Beals (ed.). Ottawa: Department of Energy, Mines and Resources

ORMSBY, MARGARET A. 1958. *British Columbia: a History*. Toronto: Macmillan Company of Canada

SOURCES

PINCOTT, K. E. 1932. 'What Churchill Owes to a Woman'. *The Beaver*, September 1932. 263:2. pp. 100–103

PINKERTON, ROBERT E. 1932. *Hudson's Bay Company*. London: Thorton Butterworth Ltd

PRESTON, RICHARD J. 1984?. 'The Witiko: Algonkian Knowledge and White Man Knowledge'. In *Myth*, pp. 111–27

QUINN, DAVID B. 1979. *New American World. Vol. III–IV*. New York: Arno Press

REY, LOUIS. 1984. 'The Evangelization of the Arctic in the Middle Ages: Gardar, the "Diocese of Ice"'. *Arctic*, December 1984. 37:4. pp. 324–33

RICH, E.E. (ed.). 1945. *Minutes of the Hudson's Bay Company 1679–1684*. First Part. London: The Hudson's Bay Record Society

RICH, E.E. (ed.). 1946. *Minutes of the Hudson's Bay Company 1679–1684*. Second Part. London: The Hudson's Bay Record Society

RICH, E.E. (ed.) 1948. *Copy-Book of Letters Outward &c Begins 29th May, 1680 Ends 5 July, 1687*. Toronto: The Champlain Society

RICH, E.E. and Johnson, A.M. (eds.). 1949. *James Isham's Observations on Hudsons Bay, 1743. And Notes and Observations on a book entitled A Voyage to Hudsons Bay in the Dobbs Galley, 1749*. London: The Hudson's Bay Record Society

RICH, E.E. (ed.). 1957. *Hudson's Bay Copy Booke of Letters Commissions Instructions Outward 1688–1696*. London: The Hudson's Bay Record Society

RICH, E.E. 1958. *Hudson's Bay Company 1670–1870, Volume One 1670–1763*. London: The Hudson's Bay Record Society

RICH, E.E. 1967. *The Fur Trade and the Northwest to 1857*. Toronto: McClelland and Stewart

RICH, E.E. 1971. 'The Road to Cathay and the Hudson's Bay Company'. *The Polar Record*, January 1971. 15:97. pp. 453–62

ROBSON, JOSEPH. 1752. *An Account of Six Years Residence in Hudson's–Bay, From 1733 to 1736, and 1744 to 1747*. London: J. Payne and J. Bouquet

ROSS, W. GILLIES and Barr, W. 1972. 'Voyages in North-western Hudson Bay (1720–1772) and Discovery of the Knight Relics on Marble Island'. *Musk-Ox*, No 11, 1972, pp. 28–33

ROSS, W. GILLIES. 1973. 'Whaling in Hudson Bay'. *The Beaver*, Summer 1973. pp. 40–7

RUGGLES, RICHARD I. 1991. *A Country so Interesting: the Hudson's Bay Company and two centuries of mapping, 1660–1870.* McGill-Queen's University Press

SCOTT, J.M. 1977. *Icebound: Journey to the Northwest Sea*. London: Gordon & Cremonesi

SMITH, ADAM. 1939. *An Inquiry into the Nature and Causes of The Wealth of Nations.* New York: The Modern Library

SMITH, RALPH. 1970. Marble Island: A Search for the Knight Expedition (August 6–15, 1970). (Unpublished report)

SMITH, RALPH. 1971. Discovery of one of James Knight's ships at Marble Island: a preliminary report. (Unpublished report)

SMITH, RALPH and Barr, William. 1971. 'A Search for the Knight expedition August 6–15, 1970. *Musk-Ox*, No. 8, 1971. pp. 40–6

SMITH, RALPH and Barr, William. 1971. 'Record of the Sloop 'Churchill's visit to Marble Island in 1787'. *Musk-Ox*, No. 9, 1971. p. 53

SMITH, RALPH. 1972. 'Relics of James Knight'. *The Beaver*, Spring 1972. 302:4. pp. 36–41

[SWIFT, JONATHAN]. 1727. *Travels Into Several Remote Nations of the World. In Four Parts. By Lemuel Gulliver.* London: Motte

TUTTLE, CHARLES R. 1885. *Our North Land: Being a full account of the Canadian North-west and Hudson's Bay Route, together with a Narrative of the Experiences of the Hudson's Bay Expedition of 1884.* Toronto: C. Blackett Robinson

TYRRELL, J.B. 1906. Description of Marble Island, Hudson Bay. Geological Survey of Canada, New Series of Annual Reports I–XVI, 1885–1906

TYRRELL, J.B. 1911. 'Editor's introduction': *A Journey From Prince of Wales's Fort in Hudson's Bay to the Northern Ocean.* Toronto: The Champlain Society

TYRRELL, J.B. (ed.). 1931. *Documents Relating to the Early History of Hudson Bay.* Toronto: The Champlain Society

UMFREVILLE, EDWARD. 1790. *The Present State of Hudson's Bay*. London: Charles Stalker

VAN KIRK, SYLVIA. 1974. 'Thanadelthur'. *The Beaver*, Spring 1974. Outfit 304:4 pp. 40–5

WARKENTIN, JOHN and Ruggles, Richard. I. 1970. *Manitoba Historical Atlas, A Selection of Facsimile Maps, Plans, and Sketches from 1612 to 1969*. Winnipeg: The Historical and Scientific Society of Manitoba

WALLIS, HELEN. 1984. 'England's Search for the Northern Passages in the Sixteenth and Early Seventeenth Centuries'. *Arctic*, December 1984. 37:4. pp. 453–72

WHYMPER, FREDERICK. 1875. *Heroes of the Arctic*. London: Society for Promoting Christian Knowledge

WILLIAMS, GLYNDWR. 1959. 'Arthur Dobbs and Joseph Robson: New Light on the Relationship Between Two Early Critics of the Hudson's Bay Company'. *Canadian Historical Review*, XL (1959). pp. 132–6

WILLIAMS, GLYNDWR. 1962. *The British Search for the Northwest Passage in the Eighteenth Century*. London: The Royal Commonwealth Society/Longmans

WILLIAMS, GLYNDWR. 1970. 'The Hudson's Bay Company and Its Critics in the Eighteenth Century'. Trans. of the Royal Historical Society, 5th Series, Vol. 20

WILLIAMSON, JAMES A. 1929. *The Voyages of the Cabots and the English Discovery of North America Under Henry VII and Henry VIII*. London: The Argonaut Press

WILLSON, BECKLES. 1900. *The Great Company 1667–1871*. London: Smith, Elder & Co.

WILSON, J. TUZO. 1949. 'New Light on Hearne'. *The Beaver*, June 1949. pp. 14–18

ZACHARCHUK, WALTER. 1973. 'The House That Knight Built'. *The Beaver*, Autumn 1973. 304:2 pp. 12–15

INDEX

Moor, William, 82, 83, 85
Moose Factory, 22, 23
Morton, Arthur S., 50, 150
Munk, Jens, 10, 60, 63

Ne Ultra, 10, 11, 71
Northwest Passage
  earlier attempts to find, 7-8,
    9-11, 28, 54, 63, 80
  subsequent attempts to find,
    82, 85, 151-2
Norton, Moses, 85-7, 140, 150,
  151-2, 155-6
Norton, Richard, 57, 61, 62-3,
  76-7, 87, 166

Palfrey, Don, 144, 145, 146
Prince of Wales's Fort, 61-2, 63,
  76, 85, 153-4

Quartzite Island, 106, 108,
  117, 142

Rankin, John, 82
Robson, Joseph, 67, 79, 155
Roe's Welcome, 71, 82
ruined shelter, 14, 89, 90, 121-5

Schwatka, Frederick, 112, 164
Scroggs, John
  account of expedition's fate,
    78, 97, 162-3
  conclusions attacked by
    Hearne, 97, 156
  disappearance of journal, 81
  discovers remains of
    expedition, 77-8, 81,
    96-7, 147
scurvy, 63, 110, 119, 134
Sergeant, Henry, 21, 23
ships
  damage theory, 140
  evidence of dismantling,
    142-3, 145-6, 147
  Hearne's account of, 139-40,
    144, 148

remains found on land,
  78, 81, 90
underwater investigation,
  139, 143-7
wintering theory, 141-2
Smith, Francis, 83, 84, 85,
  96, 167
Staunton, Richard, 76, 77,
  123, 166
Stevens, Joseph, 1-2, 89-90, 91-2,
  93, 127, 128-9, 137, 140-1, 142,
  143, 150
storage tent, possible site of, 104
Strait of Anian, 66, 71, 72, 79
Stuart, William, 42, 49-50, 69

teeth, 136-7
Thanadelthur, 37, 42, 50-1,
  57-8, 167
Thule, 117-18
Treaty of Ryswick, 30
Treaty of Utrecht, 31
Tyrrell, J. B., 155

University of Alberta expedition
  discovery of artefacts, 125-30
  discovery of bone fragments
    and teeth, 130-1, 133, 134-7
  excavation of Knight's
    shelter, 120-5
  forensic archaeology, 11,
    12-13, 99, 100
  journeys to Marble Island, 6,
    13-14, 101-2
  phases, 100-1
  search for graves, 103-4,
    118-19
  team members, 100
  test pits excavated, 120-1, 134
  underwater examination of
    ships, 139, 143-7

Vaughan, David, 45, 69, 70, 71,
  72, 144, 166

INDEX

Walker, James, 88-9
whaling, 102, 108, 110, 112, 163
Whymper, Frederick, 97, 149
Williams, Glyndwr, 71-2

York Fort, 23, 29, 30, 31, 34-5,
   38, 41-2, 43-5, 46-8, 56,
   58-60, 124
York Journal, 34, 71

ACKNOWLEDGEMENTS

First and foremost the assistance provided by the keeper and staff of the Hudson's Bay Company Archives, Provincial Archives of Manitoba, is gratefully acknowledged. Special thanks are due Anne Morton for her valued contribution.

Thanks are also due to the staffs of the following institutions. In Canada: the Bruce Peel Special Collections Library, University of Alberta; the Canadian Circumpolar Institute Library, University of Alberta; the National Archives of Canada; the National Library of Canada; the Provincial Archives of Alberta; the City of Edmonton Public Library. In Britain: the National Maritime Museum; the British Library; the Public Record Office. In the United States: the Kendall Whaling Museum and the State Department of Cultural Resources, Archives and Records Section, State of North Carolina.

We would like to express our gratitude to Professor Glyndwr Williams, who read the manuscript and provided valuable comments. Professor I. S. MacLaren kindly read the chapter entitled A Gothic Journey, and likewise provided valued comments. Manitoba North National Historic Sites, Canadian Parks Service, provided assistance related to Prince of Wales's Fort.

The Knight Project: Martin Amy, archaeological field assistant, 1989, 1990; Dr Owen Beattie, principal investigator, 1989, 1990, 1991, 1992; Andy Cameron, technical adviser, 1992; Bill Gawor, expedition assistant, 1989, 1990, 1991, 1992; John Geiger, historical investigator, 1989, 1990, 1991; Dr K. Warren Geiger, project geologist, 1990; Jeff Gilmour, diver, 1992; Feliks Kappi, student field assistant, 1989, 1990, 1991, 1992; Jennifer Kowal, camp manager, 1991; Walt Kowal, project archaeologist, 1990, 1991; Yin Lam, archaeological field assistant, 1991; Don Palfrey, diver, 1991, 1992; Warren Palfrey, student field assistant, 1991, 1992; Barb Schweger, Arctic clothing specialist, 1990,

1991; Professor Brian Spencely, archaeological field assistant, 1990, 1991; David Tatuiini, student field assistant, 1989, 1990.

Thanks also to Lavinia Brown, Ron Brown and Leonie Kappi. Additional assistance was provided by Susan Baker, Marla Limousin and Bette Palfrey.

Finally, we would like to express our appreciation to the people of Rankin Inlet, who, with friendliness and enthusiasm, made us feel we were part of their community during our brief summer stopovers.

Additional acknowledgements of John Geiger:

Thanks to A. L. Gilchrist and S. F. Keen, who started it all; Mechthild Borsch, for her mind and spirit; Victor Spinetti for the look beyond the mirrors; Bill Gawor, David Staples and Peter Hoggett for their kind assistance; and Steve Hume for his advice and inspiration. Special thanks also to Lucinda Vardey, Carolyn Brunton and the *Edmonton Journal.*

Additional acknowledgements of Owen Beattie:

Primary funding for the field and laboratory research was provided by the Social Sciences and Humanities Research Council of Canada (1991, 1992). Initial funding was provided by the Boreal Institute for Northern Studies (1989). Additional aid, support and encouragement came from the University of Alberta (1990), Rolex (1990), Canadian Airlines International (1990), the Brick (1990), the Churchill Corporation (1990), Northwest Territorial Airlines (1992), Economic Development and Tourism - Rankin Inlet (1991, 1992), and Sinniktarvik (1991, 1992). I would like to extend my sincere thanks to these organizations and agencies for making the research possible. Thanks to Aquarius Flight, Inc. of Markham, Ontario, and R. Bolivar (photographer) and G. Spurrell (pilot), for aerial photographs of Marble and Quartzite Islands. I am also grateful to my friend Roger Amy for encouragement and ideas for the project.